G. L. (George Loftus) Tottenham

Terence McGowan

The Irish Tenant

G. L. (George Loftus) Tottenham

Terence McGowan
The Irish Tenant

ISBN/EAN: 9783744760393

Printed in Europe, USA, Canada, Australia, Japan

Cover: Foto ©ninafisch / pixelio.de

More available books at **www.hansebooks.com**

TERENCE McGOWAN,

THE IRISH TENANT.

By G. L. TOTTENHAM.

IN TWO VOLUMES.

VOL. II.

> "And here and there, as up the crags you spring,
> Mark many rude-carved crosses near the path;
> Yet deem not these devotion's offering—
> These are memorials frail of murderous wrath,
> * * * * *
> And grove and glen with thousand such are rife
> Throughout this purple land, where law secures not life."

LONDON:
SMITH, ELDER & CO., 15, WATERLOO PLACE.
1870.

[THE RIGHT OF TRANSLATION IS RESERVED.]

TERENCE McGOWAN,

THE IRISH TENANT.

CHAPTER I.

There were sounds of autumn in the waning woods; the beeches were in their first brilliant stage of orange-brown; the mountain ash in the glen hung their scarlet clusters amid yellowing and falling leaves; the nuts that were yet unpicked by Sunday boys and girls were dropping from their husks among the hazel copses and along the hill-side rock; the reeds upon the lochs contrasting brightly with the calm blue waters in the frosty morning air; and the golden sunrise had already flushed the first streak of snow on the top of Thor.

The political agitation of the county had reached its height: the riotous spirits were worked up to full fighting pitch: the seething ferment of excitement which had brought all classes under its influence during the last few weeks was about to boil over; there was but one topic of conversation—the election; and the dreaded day had antepenultimately arrived. All the respectable part of the community were longing for it to be over, apprehending even worse scenes of tumult and popular disturbance than had disgraced the electoral humanity of the county at the last contested election; deploring the gross misuse of their power and position which had characterized the action of the priests; regretting the lamentable insufficiency of polling-places, which gave every opportunity for the organization of mob-violence and intimidation, and almost thinking that it was better that the county should not have a member at all, than that his election should be the occasion of reviving so much bitter party feeling and political animosity, which would not subside again for months, and even years after, as they knew, by experience of the last contest. Spiritual intimidation had been carried to such a pitch, that the Roman Catholic bishop of the diocese had even threatened to cut off from the sacraments of the church, and refuse admittance to the chapel, any member of his flock who voted contrary to his directions. The priests in the several parishes—notably the Rev. Patrick Maguire, P.P.—had preached the most violent abuse of landlords and Conservatives from the altar; and pressed on the one side by their clergy, and on the other by their landlords, the unfortunate electors hardly knew which way to turn, and cursed the evil hour in which they had been entrusted with a vote. Conservative voters had been kidnapped, bullied, told by their spiritual conscience-keepers that whatever promises they might have given to Lord Shirley were not binding upon them. Some had been bribed to absent themselves from the county on the day of voting; others had been beaten, had their houses wrecked, and their property carried off; while it was confidently reported that such mobs had been hired by the Radical candidate, that neither at Kilmorris, which was the principal polling-place, nor at Kiltyfarnham, at the other end, would the Conservatives have a chance of ever coming to the poll. Troops had been massed at either place, large bodies of constabulary brought in from adjoining counties, two extra stipendaries sent down; and yet even so the townspeople looked forward to the day with the utmost dread, having already had one or two foretastes of the riotous scenes they might expect, when the mob-supporters of Brady's side had made displays through the town on market-days. Every sort of libel and calumny had been invented and uttered by Brady against his opponent. His son even had been beaten by one of that side; and according to his speeches, there was no outrage which they had not attempted, no device to which they had not had recourse, to cripple the freedom of action of his supporters. But he confidently asserted that he would be triumphant notwithstanding, and recommended Lord Shirley to withdraw, and not bring upon himself the responsibility of the bloodshed which would otherwise, he believed, ensue.

Lord Shirley, however, did not retire, but had guards mounted over his voters in remote districts, brought others down to Mount-Stewart, engaged every conveyance in the county that was not under orders for the priests, winked at a liberal supply of whiskey in necessary quarters, and looked forward with confidence to a large majority, provided that anything like the number of votes which he had been promised were actually polled.

The nomination day was over, and a sufficiently riotous exhibition of passion and violence there had been. Shirley was calm and dignified—however inwardly disagreeable he might have found it facing a demonstratively yelling mob of Irishmen, whose ready wit and ridicule were as disconcerting as their more substantial interruptions—while Mr. Brady's large and coarse appearance was rendered yet more unattractive by the abusive manner in which he pointed at and discussed his opponent, who was sitting within a few yards of his shouting point. The show of hands was, of course, ten to one in his favour; and when he had a mob hired for the express purpose of standing under the hustings and hooting down Shirley and cheering himself, it would have been hard if he could not have had this gratifying show of triumph. In the evening his party paraded the streets in defiance of police and military, broke the windows of obnoxious Conservatives, listened with tumultuous applause to seditious harangues from violent political priests, and didn't go home till morning—till the streets were swept by dragoons, and the inhabitants thereby allowed a few hours relief from the terror of momentary invasion or destruction.

At Geraldscourt the utmost excitement prevailed, and Lady Eleanor hardly slept at night from thinking what a disgrace it would be to the Conservatives of the county if the priests returned their man. Nora cared little for the political element in the contest, but a great deal for the danger which she knew to be abroad in the present state of party feeling in the county. Every day she expected to hear that Lord Shirley had fallen a victim to the violence of the people; and whenever her father left home to be present at any meeting, or indeed to go outside the place at all, she was never happy until he was again under his own roof. Familiarity ought to have diminished her fears, but the turbulent spirit which had been let loose was daily accredited with wilder and more outrageous acts; and the prominent part which, at his mother's instigation, Alan was taking in the Conservative interest, made her tremble for his safety if a collision should occur. To-day—the antepenultimate, as we said, of the polling-day—he had gone off in the morning to Kilmorris to bring back an escort of soldiers for his voters, who were all to assemble the following afternoon at Geraldscourt, stay there the night, and be conveyed *en masse* to the poll the day after.

Lady Eleanor had been restlessly awaiting his return all the afternoon, and directly he arrived, she hurried into the hall, and informed him that Bartley Mc Loughlin (the bailiff) had been down with news that a party of Brady's men from Corranmore were coming down that very night to sweep the country up to Ballyduff, and carry off every voter into the mountains.

"Now, I'll tell you what you'll do," she went on; "take Terence Mc Gowan (I've sent over for him), and Larry, and Pat Connor, and Bartley, and be beforehand with them. Bring them all with you down here into the yard this evening; I'll see that the soldiers are attended to, and there are gallons of whiskey in the house. You haven't any time to lose."

Seeing that it was already getting dark, Alan laughingly agreed with her, but never thought of declining the expedition she had planned for him. There was something wild and adventurous about it which enlisted his sympathy at once.

"I knew it was just the sort of work you would like," Lady Eleanor said. "Don't come into collision with the others if it can be avoided—we want votes, not fighting. Just introduce this young man"—signifying a cornet of dragoons, who was clanking into the hall at the moment—"and then see Bartley at once. I'm not sure whether Terence and Larry have arrived yet or not; they had not a quarter of an hour ago."

The military youth had arrived within introduction distance by this time, and Alan introduced "Mr. Glenboy," or "Lord Glenboy, I should say," he added, laughing.

The youngster made his bow, and Lady Eleanor gave him what he thought, considering his importance (at the present time particularly), a very unceremonious welcome. She was never very partial to young military gentlemen, and at the present moment much too preoccupied with election prospects to evince an interest in his uniform which she didn't feel.

"Mr. Rochfort is obliged to go away at once to secure some of our voters," she said; "but I hope we shall be able to make you comfortable in his absence, Mr. Glenboy. He has already given orders about accommodation for your men. I don't much think we shall require their services to-night; but really, with the country in such a state, there's no knowing what may not be attempted."

Glenboy thought a siege would be rather good fun, and made some further remarks about the general expectation of a row, referring particularly to the very uninteresting part which he and his comrades would be compelled to play on the occasion; and Alan hurried off to see Bartley, and find out how far his information might be correct.

Bartley McLoughlin was sitting in the kitchen at the time, entertaining the maids with the dry expression in which it was his custom to vent his thoughts. He was a stoutish, short, keen-eyed, and sometimes spectacled old man—with a face like unto a carp's face, or the algebraic sign which is used to denote "greater than," if the dim reminiscences of algebraic days do not mislead my pen. A very large and loosely made frieze-coat entailed his person, and gave a portly dignity to the shrewdness of his face. It was supposed that no man had ever got to the bottom of Bartley Mc Loughlin, and it was a proved certainty that no one man had ever been too many for him on the surface. He had been bailiff on the Geraldscourt estate since far back into the reign of Alan's father; and thanks to the leniency with which the property was administered, he could ride home at night with a feeling of tolerable security. Of course he was obliged now and then to impound a pig or cow, or other animal of domestic use, in order to enforce payment of rent for meeting the inevitable interest of mortgages; but he was too old an institution to be shot, and application to the landlord generally had the desired result of releasing the object of his attentions for the time being. He had a way, too, of keeping in with the people which was not altogether, perhaps, in his master's interest, but suited very well the general laxness of management, and conduced towards peace and quietness upon the property. Rochfort knew as well as he did himself that tenants were very often doing what they had no right to do—breaking covenants, cutting timber, bog, &c., where they had no business to cut them; and so long as *he* didn't mind, and said nothing, why should Bartley make enemies for himself by drawing his attention more particularly to the offending point. Obviously that would have been mere officiousness on his part. Otherwise he was perfectly honest; never received a bribe or bonus for his good word, and feathered his nest quietly and surely from only legitimate sources. Such was the individual who was to be seen, at least once or twice in the week, hanging about the office-door, with his riding-stick in his hand, silently appraising each new comer and his errand, and who now gave Rochfort very good authority for the information which he had brought.

"Have Terence and Larry come yet?"

Not yet, though a "soople gorsoon" had been despatched for them.

"Pat Connor's below," Bartley said, taking a pinch of snuff. It's a pity that it isn't possible to convey a notion even of the deliberate desiccated absence of express meaning with which that pinch of snuff was taken. Whether he meant thereby to announce the fact in connection with the mention of the others who were to be of their party; whether he meant to say that Pat Connor was a host in himself; whether he meant to say that they had better start at once—that they required no further support; or whether he meant nothing more than met the ear it would be impossible to determine, and on the whole, perhaps, is not worth considering.

"We'll give them a few minutes longer," said Rochfort; "it's just as well to be prepared, in case we should fall in with these Corranmore boys."

"That's true then; it's not the day the high wind comes to be goin' lookin' for the slates," rejoined Bartley, with sententious indifference.

Pat Connor was summoned; stout blackthorns were selected; Rochfort's revolver was stowed away into his pocket; and just as they were about to start Terence and Larry, with kippeens apiece, appeared out of the darkness, and they set out together upon their wild expedition.

By the time they had cleared the demesne it was dark night, and a very dark night to boot; the wind rising and carrying them before it every now and then, as it swept past in strong rushing gusts, and moaning away down the hollows in a very wild and dismal fashion. It was a good thing, Alan thought, that they had Terence and Larry with them, knowing the country as they did; crossing a mountain on such a night without experienced guides would be no very safe proceeding, even if it was so with them.

The darkness and the wildness of the night had some effect upon the conversation, and there were pauses every now and then, while they walked rapidly on, as if they had just as soon get their work over as quickly as possible.

During one of these pauses they were all unpleasantly startled in a pretty equal degree by hearing a voice suddenly come out of the darkness close in front of them.

"It's a fine night;" and a man passed them on the grass at the side at the same time. There was no immediate answer from any of the party. They all knew well enough what these words meant. It was the Ribbonman's sign.

The password might have been known by some of them; but to give it in their present company was out of the question. "The moon's up," for instance, would have been about as inapplicable to existing circumstances as the original assertion that it was a fine night; and so the salutation was merely acknowledged, and they passed on with an uncomfortable feeling which the darkness had not produced before. How did they know whether that man was alone or not, or what work might be on for the night? Rochfort instinctively felt for his revolver, and the others grasped their blackthorns with a tighter grip, and spoke in lower tones. A few moments after their hearts again beat quicker as they heard the measured tread of feet approaching; but this time they were relieved to find it was policemen, fully armed, patrolling. They were pressed into the service, and their front was now a pretty formidable one as they struck across the bog-road leading to Ballyduff, intending to commence at the further end of their beat first. There was no sign of a star; the only light to be seen was the glimmerings from cottage windows, where the families were sitting over the fire with close-barred doors, imagining superstitious voices in the howlings of the wind, or dreading lest their houses should be stripped and left roofless before the morning. Will-o'-the-wisps danced with a wild weird light across the bog, and close along the road. The shriek of the snipe was carried past upon the gale, and dark forms flitting every now and then across the path awakened much stranger imaginations than the sight of a hare in daylight would suggest.

"There's a place where I had the narrowest escape I ever had in my life of being drowned," said Rochfort, as they came to a spot where the dark water could be darkly seen on either side of the bankless road. "It was on a night very like this itself. Barney, the rascal, had been making too good use of his time in Ballyduff, and as soon as we got well away from the turn—he kept quiet enough until then—his spirits began to rise, and away he went as if it was driving a race he was, whooping and shouting and holding on by the mare's mouth and wondering why she wouldn't go on at all. And not a bit of him would he give up the reins, so we just had to take our chance; and a bad one it was, when I found the wheel hanging over the side of that ditch there. To this day I cannot make out how we got back into the road at all. Devil a step further would I let him drive me then, but just made him sit on his seat, or walk beside me if he liked it better, while I led the car the rest of the way down. It would have done you good to see the shameface he had on him the next day after. He took the pledge and kept it ever since, I believe."

"I heard that," said the sergeant.

"He was a funny chap then when he'd had his glass," said Larry.

"That's what he was, Larry, and no mistake," said Rochfort; "if it hadn't been that I was in fear of my life every minute, I'd have been killed with laughing at him that very night. It was the bad whiskey they gave him that upset him, he said."

"Indeed, the stuff that's sold in the country is enough to upset any man that'll take a couple of glasses of it," said Terence, "for it's little better than poison it is. Some say there's more vitriol a good deal and medicine of one kind or another than spirits in it. It's enough to burn the inside out of a man, and abuse him al-together."

"There was a young chap," said the sergeant, "that was servant to one of these publicans one time, sir, told me himself that, after a fair day was over, the man that owned the whiskey would just take what was left of it and turn the tap and let it run out into the yard away; that he wouldn't think of putting his lips to it himself at all."

"But what are your excise people doing," asked Rochfort, "that they don't look after them?"

"Ah! it isn't easy coming at them at all; when an officer 'll come in there'll always be a good glass for him, and only that he'd take them unawares as a poor country fellow, he'd never convict. It's not to be wondered at, sir, that there's fighting and rows in the country when people's heads are set mad with that kind of drink."

"There was a publican fellow came to Dr. Fludyer one time," said Bartley, "and asked him for a quantity of strong stuff that he used reg'lar for medicine. I don't mind what's this the name of it was. But Dr. Fludyer asked him, what did he want it for.

"'To make potheen with,' says he.

"'And is that what you give the counthry people for whiskey?' says the doctor.

"'The very same,' he says, 'with plenty of spring water mixed, and maybe a spoonful or two of the stuff, just to give it a taste, d'ye see.'

"So it wasn't too long after that that the doctor had some chaps at work haymaking, and what does he do, but he takes a quart of spring water and mixes with it a sup o' the medicine and a wee drop of potheen, and sends it out to the boys in the field.

"'Well, boys,' he says, coming out presently, 'was that good potheen ye got?'

"'To be sure,' they said, 'it was.'

"'Well, now, I'll just tell ye,' he said, 'there wasn't more than a wineglassful in the whole of it,' and he tells them then, giving out the right thing at the same time, how he come to make it; 'and boys,' he says, 'if you take my advice you'll never drink a glass of whiskey in a public-house at all, for what you got just now is the very best that ever ye'll get.' So he just told them that."

"I think there's not much whisky drank in these parts at all, your honour," said Terence. "Father Hugh has the most of them, in this parish, teetotallers altogether. He's very much against drink entirely; and there's one thing, he says, and I agree with him in that, that a man 'll surely have no chance for his soul in the next world if he'll die in intoxication. And if a person 'll not attend to these things, it'll not go well with him, there's no second question about it."

"Father Hugh is not half the politician Father Maguire is," said Rochfort.

"He is not, sir, at all," said the sergeant, "he's a very quiet man, and a very religious man, and has done a great deal of good among the people, and keeps them very well regulated. It's only when an election comes round that he takes any part at all in political matters; and party business he won't allow at all, for, he says, it's against the law of God and the law of the land both. There are wild chaps, of course, that'll go their own way in spite of him or any man, but the most of the young fellows in his parish go to their duty regularly once a month; and isn't that a great thing for him to say?"

"Did you hear, your honour, how Barney played off Father Maguire the other day when he was married?" asked Pat Connor.

"I did not, Pat; how was that?"

"Well, he went, and he asked him first how much would it take to marry him, and Father Maguire tells him that he knows he'll have a good bit of money with the girl he was goin' to marry, and he must pay him two pounds, no less.

"'Ah!' says Barney, 'sure your riverence wouldn't be so hard upon a poor man?'

"'Well, it's not a poor man you'd be at all,' says the priest, 'if you were not the big spender you are. Two pounds it must be, Barney, or you'll not get married by me, and you'll be whistlin' for the fortune that's comin' to you.'

"So Barney began to play with him then, and said that maybe he'd get it done cheaper by some other man. His reverence didn't agree to that at all, and just told him that for his impudence now he'd be to pay another pound, and not a sixpence less than three would he take.

" 'Well, I'm sorry for that, your riverence,' says Barney; 'for I'd have liked to let yourself have the job. I'll be forced to go now to the county M'yo, where I'll get a cousin o' my own that'll do it for nothin'; ' and he off with him then to the cousin, comin' back a week after with the wife and the fortune."

"No fear but Barney's the boy knows how to fit the priest," said Bartley; and it was generally agreed that Barney undoubtedly was such a boy.

Further conversation was here interrupted by the inequalities of the mountain track upon which they had entered, and they proceeded through bog and darkness and stormy wind as best they could until the first house was reached.

There was no answer at first to the summons, but a cessation of voices within; and Larry looked in through the fire-lighted window, and asked, "Are ye there, Tierney?"

The sound of many feet without had evidently produced an uncomfortable impression, and an old man's voice inquired in Irish from the other side of the door, what it was at all they wanted.

Bartley's reply, also in Irish, seemed to reassure him a little, and the door was cautiously unbarred, and Rochfort admitted.

There was no time for much explanation, a long stretch of country having yet to be travelled; and the bewildered old man had to come away without even a tooth-brush for his toilet on the following morning. He had no English, or scarcely any, this old remnant of less locomotive days, and he and Bartley continued to converse unintelligibly in Irish for some distance, until Rochfort broke in to compliment the latter on the greater fluency of expression which he appeared to have in his native tongue.

It would be a strange thing, Bartley said, if a man wouldn't be able to speak the language of his country that he was born to, and it was a mighty big pity that it was falling into disuse in the country. The priest even had given over preaching in Irish, and there were many young fellows growing up that couldn't speak it at all; and to Bartley's mind, it was a disgrace to them. He himself was reckoned a first-rate Irish scholar, one of the best; and he had an Irish MS. in his family that he was very proud of, which was nearly two hundred years old, as he was wont to declare.

Irish was not only a beautiful language, he said (this was the only topic upon which he could ever be drawn into much expression); but it was a very ancient language, and a language of itself, "and that's more nor the English can boast, I'm thinkin'."

"You'll find mixture enough there any way," said Rochfort.

"Did you ever hear tell, your honour, how the English lord came over the Irish lord in the Parliament one time, when there was a talk of throwin' overboard the Irish language? The Irish lord was for supportin' the language of his country, and the English lord was for throwin' it overboard; and at last the English lord says to the Irish lord, 'Will you Irish me "raw egg" now, till we see what kind of a language it is that ye're for upholdin'?' and that was the most contrairy word he could give him in the whole language.

"'Ough ow!' says the Irish lord; and the English

fellow turns round then, and says, 'Isn't that a pretty language now, that's just like the bark of a dog?' so the English fellow was too much for him then, and the Irish language was thrown overboard."

"Well, it isn't often, Bartley, the Englishman 'll get the best of it with an Irishman, for all they think so much of themselves."

"I'm thinkin' that, indeed," said Bartley.

"Well, indeed, it's not right, then," he continued, "to let go a language as ancient as it; that was spoke at the Tower of Babbel, by all account; and it's clear that Adam himself spoke it too; an' I'll tell ye the reason o' that: When all the birds and the beasts were brought to him to give names to them, d'ye see, he gave this to one and that to another, and so on until the turn of the ass came. Adam then saw the lad comin' up to him, and he saw that he was a disobedient kind of a chap; and he called him 'assule'—that's disobedient; and *assal* is the very name we give to the ass in Irish now, without goin' the rounds to call him *assule*."

"Usen't they tell fine stories, Bartley, some

o' the old men in these parts, about the greatness, and the manhood, and the bravery of the Irish giants that used to be formerly?" asked another of the party, leading up to Bartley's lore, which always found due appreciation in the love of scholarship and learning natural to Irishmen. (3)

"To be sure they did," said Bartley. "Such stories you wouldn't begrudge sitting up the whole night listenin' to them—about Finn-ma-Caul, and Gul, and many more besides; so interesting they were, and all about the *e*-vents of former times. St. Patrick, they say, was once talkin' to some man about God, and the glory and the power of the Omnipotent Being, and says he, 'Well, if I'd see him wrastle with Gul, and he'd toss him, then I'd believe every word ye're tellin' me;' so you see *he* put Gul before God."

The termination of Bartley's anecdote found them at the door of Owen, the mountain-keeper's cottage. He was not a voter, but might be a useful attendant, in virtue of his strong right arm. They found him in the first-day fury of indignation against some person unknown, who had cut off the tails of two of his cows on the previous night; and he somewhat unreasonably, not being a voter, set down the outrage to some of Brady's party, who had been threatening to beat him on the last fair day for his loudly expressed hostility to their side.

"Well now, there's not another reason for it but the one that I'm tellin' ye" he asserted, when Rochfort declined to believe that political spite could have gone so far. "And there's more nor myself served the same way." It was none of the neighbours, he could swear, for he never had any disagreements or law suits with one of them; he was an advocate of peace and quietness himself; "and it's very few neighbours," he said, "but must trouble other some time in the year, whether it's about a pass, or a ditch, or a trespass, or somethin', so that it 'd be too bad for a man to be always havin' his horn out strivin' to cut a hole in him."

Hesiod would have been charmed with his neighbourly sentiments.

If he could only "get him in hoults," the man that done it, Owen said, he'd let him know what it was worth to harm a poor man in that fashion.

The sergeant had only heard of it that evening, and therefore, as he said, had not been able to scrutinize the matter as yet; but it was his opinion that it must have been some of Brady's party who had done that, and burnt another man's hayrick in the next townland also.

"They say he's offered land at scarce a rent at all to some of them, if they'll vote for him," said Bartley.

"Oh! well, they needn't think it'd last long at that," said Terence. "He'd soon enough have a big rise on them after."

"I hear he's ruining himself with all the money he's spending in whiskey and other ways," said the serjeant.

"Divil thank him, for it's he can afford it," said another.

"Begor, it should be any way," added a third, "with the rents he's gettin' in Carrickamore. Ah! he's a bad man."

By this time the party had grown to a goodly number. Some had been pulled out of bed; others frightened out of their lives at the sound of visitors at that time of night, but all happy enough to escape the alternative of falling into the hands of the boys from Corranmore, looking forward to much whiskey for the next two nights at Geraldscourt, and finding a fresh fund for jokes and laughter at each new house they came to.

Across the hill, then, to Phelim Mc Gowan's, and as the lights from the post-office at Geraldsbridge glimmered into sight through the darkness, the wind came rushing up the glen upon them laden with a wild uproar of broken shouts and laughter from the village through which they had to pass on their return. Many of the party were conscious of turning pale—the whiskey was going round freely below, it was easy to tell that; the fighting instinct started up at once in others, and it was with quite a thrill of adventurous glee that Rochfort hurried forward to make sure of the two or three voters that were left before the other party could anticipate them.

Now Phelim Mc Gowan, and Phelim Mc Gowan's wife too, had been much exercised in spirit about this necessity of voting with their landlord, and it was only this very day that Father Maguire had accompanied Father Hugh to represent to Mrs. Mc Gowan's superstitious view the hideous consequences which were likely to ensue if her husband voted contrary to the wishes of his clergy.

Terence had heard nothing of the visit, but Mrs. Mc Gowan had been sadly troubled in heart ever since, and had determined that, come what would, Phelim should not vote at this election. The consequence was that, when the rescue-party arrived, poor Phelim was found doubled up with pain in bed, very like Gil Blas in the robbers' cave, while his wife was wringing her hands over him, and begging him by everything that she held most sacred not to leave her alone in the wide world.

"Oh! your honour, didn't I know when he met the red-haired woman on the road below this day that there was somethin' to happen him? and I'm afeard it's more nor a colic he took that's brought him to his bed now. What 'll he do at all with them wild fellows below, for not a stir ever he'll stir this night, as you may hear by the roars of him within."

Pale from apprehension, night-capped and dishevelled, Phelim was a sufficiently pitiable object to view as he writhed in agony on the bed. It was evident that he couldn't go with them, and as there was no time to be lost, and it was probable that the Corranmore party would find out that they had been forestalled before they got so far, they were obliged to leave him to the tender care of his distracted wife, with a promise that Terence should come up early the next morning to see after him.

Terence could not refuse to credit the tortures which his parent was ostensibly suffering, but he determined to be up with him the very first thing in the morning; and owing to the hurry they were in at the moment, had no time to probe his mother's anxiety for further particulars.

One after another the remaining voters were picked out of bed, and when the last was secured they were near enough to the village to catch distinctly the tenor of the talk which was being flung about below them to windward. Rochfort and Terence crept stealthily down there to a slight eminence in the immediate neighbourhood, and reconnoitred for a time; and bringing back word that their numbers were far superior to their own, it was determined, in consideration of the fighting power which they had been imbibing—and, as Lady Eleanor had said, votes and not broken heads being the object of the expedition—to strike off to the right and avoid them, crossing the river by the stepping-stones above.

"Whisht, now, boys, not a word!" said Rochfort, as they faced the hill again, huddled whisperingly together; and for some time they scrambled on in silence, until by the distant noise they could tell that the village party was moving on along the road they had lately quitted. Their present route was the shortest now, and still the safest, and they continued down to the road again.

The leaders had hardly emerged upon it, when they were accosted by an evident straggler from the other party with the Ribbon watchword.

Before he could find out his mistake he was secured—no jokes, however, being passed upon his capture, although he was known to some of the party, and he was carried silently away with them until they entered into the still gloomier darkness of the trees, and groped their way along down the winding path which led to the stepping-stones.

"I'm afeard, your honour, the river 'll be middlin' high," said Terence; "there fell a good share of rain last night."

"That's what I've been thinking," said Rochfort; "but, at the worst, it's easily forded."

The bank was reached, and the stepping-stones were not to be made out. The water flowed by with a cold, gurgling sound, plashing invisibly among the rocks, and the fall above had a dull, menacing roar, which made many of the dark forms clustering on the bank shrink from the thought of committing themselves to the treacherous footing of the rocks at the bottom on such a night. Even in daylight a nervous sensation, a certain notion of dim eventualities, may be felt while stumbling over rocks in midstream, with the waters sweeping by on either side. At night, when the imagination is more alive to fear, the fording of a slightly swollen river may be not at all a pleasant necessity; and if poor Nora Rochfort could only have known how her father was situated at the present moment, the suspense which she was enduring would have been heightened tenfold, if that were possible.

It was hours since he had set out; Glenboy had made an excuse to retire to his room, and even Lady Eleanor was beginning to be a little anxious, as much about Alan as about the safety of his batch of voters. The danger he was incurring there was no denying. The darkness of the night, the difficulties of the mountain paths, the scanty number of his attendants, his own reckless love of danger, and a multitude of other vague alarms, had contributed each their force to make the evening a very long and a very anxious one.

Twelve o'clock struck, and still he had not returned. Lady Eleanor put down her book and stared into the fire; and the anxious expression upon Nora's face deepened as the ringing sound of the clock drew her attention more clearly to the hour.

At that moment, as she listened more intensely for the first sign of his return, there suddenly rose upon the blast which shook the room at times, a sound which startled even Lady Eleanor, sending a sudden chill to her heart, and driving all the colour from her face.

It was a sound as of a wailing child, low and mournful at one moment, and then again borne past upon the wind with a wild, intense melancholy, which sent a shudder to the very bones; so close, so prophetic, so dismal did it sound. Nora, pale and terrified, turned to her grandmother to try and borrow some of her firmness of nerve, as she gasped, in a terrified whisper, "*The Banshee!*" but Lady Eleanor's face, too, was very pale. Had not the same supernatural warning been heard the night Alan's father was brought home a corpse? Was it not a well-authenticated tradition of the family that this dread midnight wail was always the precursor of a death? There was more than superstition here. This was one of those mysterious facts which lie beyond human grasp, but which must not on that account be contemptuously denied. Such were Lady Eleanor's feelings, and as the awful warning note, as she read it, rose and fell with that unearthly moaning measure which she so well remembered, and then died away again amid the howling and the rattling of the gust against the window-panes, she felt a sick and shuddering horror at heart, which quite incapacitated her from any attempt to administer relief or firmness to her granddaughter.

A moment after the door was hurriedly opened, and their hearts are in their mouths, as Nora's nurse bursts into the room.

"You heard it, my lady!"

Ashamed of having allowed herself to be so startled by the opening of a door, Lady Eleanor recalled her self-command at once, and answered in a low, firm voice—

"Yes, Jane, I did hear it."

She glanced at Nora as she spoke, and started up at once. "Quick, some water; don't you see she has fainted?" and in a moment her energy returned, and she was hurrying off for restoratives, leaving Nora pale and cold and motionless upon the sofa. It were better to have slept on than awake to such thoughts as hers.

"Papa—has he come back?" were the first words she uttered; and when Lady Eleanor, bending over her, said, "Not yet, my dearest child, but he will directly," she seemed for a moment about to relapse again into unconsciousness, such a terrible dread came over her.

Then there was a noise of approaching voices and steps before the front of the house; the nurse hurried away, and Lady Eleanor could see by the heaving and throbbing of her bosom that Nora had heard them, and was enduring the same throes of suspense as herself.

The nurse's face, as she hurries into the room again, reassures her.

"He has come back, Nora, safe; bear up now, and don't let him see that you have been frightened: say nothing about it. Do you hear me, Jane: don't let the subject be mentioned in Mr. Rochfort's hearing. Now go, I hear him coming. Do you think you could sit up, my child?" turning again to Nora.

"Why, mother, what has happened?" exclaimed Alan, coming into the room; "all the servants look as scared as if they had seen a ghost; and, Nora! why, my poor child, what is the matter with you too? You're as white as a sheet!"

"Oh, papa! she gasped out, "I'm so glad you have come back."

"The fact is, Alan," said Lady Eleanor, "she has worried herself into a fainting fit about you, thinking that something must have happened to you, you were so long in coming back. Try and make her believe that you are as safe as ever."

"Why of course I am, my darling child," he said, sitting down by her and taking her head upon his shoulder; "and I should have been back an hour ago if it had not been that we had a long delay about getting a prisoner across the river. We couldn't let him go on the other side, or he would have had time to join his party and intercept us; but I wouldn't for all the votes in Ireland have had my Nora frightened in this way, if I'd known that that would be the consequence."

Lady Eleanor's heart misgave her still. However great a shock to imaginary apprehensions the sudden appearance of the object of them, full of undoubted life, might be, there was still the shadow of that sickening dread remaining.

"There, cheer up, my child," continued Alan,

"and forget it all; and mother, have you been frightened too?" he asked; "you haven't even asked me what success we had."

Lady Eleanor's interest in votes and voters was no longer what it had been; but still she entered with apparent zest into his account of the night's adventures, and listened to the humorous picture he drew of the crossing of the river in single file with their prisoner tied to two of them in the middle, with all the appreciation he desired, but with an unconquerable feeling that his laughing humour was but the jarring levity of a man unconscious of the nearness of his end; and the thought produced an inexpressible sadness and depression of spirit which it was difficult to conceal.

"Where is young Glenboy," asked Alan, suddenly recollecting his existence. "Have you sent him to bed, Nora?"

"He found us rather dull, I think," said Lady Eleanor, "and pleaded a headache. The men, I believe, are satisfied with their quarters. What are you going to do with these new arrivals?"

"Oh, they'll find plenty of place to sleep about

the lofts, I daresay. At present, they are busy at whiskey, and probably will be for the next thirty-six hours, at least. Do you think you are strong enough to go upstairs now, my darling," he said, bending down over her, and kissing her, "or shall I carry you? Come, that'll be the best way, and you'll go to sleep, and forget that you were ever foolish enough to be frightened at all."

Nora had lain passively in his arms, and now, too, passively acquiesced; a slight shudder passing through her as he said the word "forget." What a clinging silent embrace as he parted from her, after leaving her to the care of her old nurse! He should look in again before going to bed, to see that she had gone to sleep, as he told her. Her nerves were evidently upset, there was such a strange sort of suppressed something in her manner which was unusual to her. However, there was nothing like a good night's rest to settle the nerves. (4)

CHAPTER II.

There were too many wants to be attended to next day to allow the household to be occupied entirely with the thoughts to which the occurrence of the previous night had given rise, but if Alan had not himself also been in a bustle of activity with soldiers, voters, and messengers of one kind or another, he could hardly have failed to notice the strange looks which were cast at him from time to time, and the sadness of alacrity with which the servants performed his orders. It had begun to be whispered about in the yard, too, and those who were not half or altogether drunk were talking together in low-voiced groups, following him with their eyes whenever he came amongst them, with the terrible interest which a man marked out for death arouses in the least superstitious mind. His unconscious cheerfulness only made the interest the more painful, and even the clanking soldiers who had caught the whispered dread, began to wish their stay was over under this death-shadowed roof.

As Terence strode along the road, at early dawn, on a confidential errand with which he had been entrusted the night before, his thoughts were a chaos of unwilling apprehensive fears. His mother's superstitious folly he always ridiculed, and wouldn't listen to or entertain at all; but there was concurrent testimony to the warning heard last night, and reason was subdued before the uncomfortable fears which were connected in his mind with the experience of all the old men upon the estate.

It was noon before his message was delivered, and then his father came into his mind once more, and he turned his steps in the direction of the cottage, over the neighbouring hill. Even at the moment as he changed his course, strange things were occurring at this same cottage.

Enraged at their disappointment, the Corranmore party had turned back without getting so far as Phelim's house the night before; and Mrs. McGowan, doubtful of being able to keep up in daylight before Terence the deception by which she had prevented Phelim from accompanying the rest on the previous night, cast about in her mind for other means which might equally secure immunity from voting. A happy plan was thought of, and had scarcely been acted upon, when who should appear coming down the road but Father Maguire, Father Hugh, and "a few boys." They were picking up straggling voters, had heard of the failure of their intended sweep the night before, and had also received information of Phelim Mc Gowan's having been left behind.

As the priests entered her cottage, Mrs. McGowan —after the manner of her sex—fell on her knees before them with superstitous awe and humility, and invoked their blessing, with much faith and dread.

"I heard Phelim was not well," said Father Hugh, while the other bent a stern eye on the woman's face, and bided his time. "Where is he?" continued Father Hugh, mildly; he was not at all the fierce, violent man his brother-priest was.

"Didn't they send up this mornin' at daylight, your riverence, and take him down to the rest at the

Big House, and him scarce able to walk? It's dead intirely he'll be, I'm afeard, before he'd get there at all."

She looked up anxiously to see if the fiction was believed; but alas! it was not.

"Sarah McGowan," said Father Maguire, perceiving that the time had now arrived for overawing the trembling victim, "that is not the case."

She trembled at their feet, and for a moment said nothing, but then burst into a torrent of assertion and gesticulation to support the statement. It was of no use, it was overdone—there was falsehood in her face.

"Sarah McGowan," thundered Father Maguire again, "listen to me. We don't believe a word you utter. Your husband must vote with us. You must tell us where he is to be found, or—" and here he raised his voice, and bent his brows, until he became the very impersonation of a terrible avenging fury,— "we turn you into a black beetle upon your own hearth—upon your own hearth, Sarah McGowan— a black BEETLE!"

He paused decisively, and the poor woman seemed

already to experience a tendency in the direction indicated, for she grovelled at their feet upon the floor, and implored them to spare her. She already felt the change beginning: her arms were growing black and diminishing in the dirt; horns—she knew it, she felt it—were at that moment starting from her head, and feelers growing out upon her sides; and she sprang to her still remaining feet, and declared that she would do anything she was bid if the threat was only recalled.

"Come, tell us, then, where he is," said Father Hugh.

"I will, your riverence, I will, indeed, I will!" and she issued from the door a picture of abject fear, and pointed to the turf-stack. Father Hugh could hardly repress a smile, but the other sternly ordered some of the boys to pull down the stack.

Half-a-dozen sods of the turf were displaced, and the top of a crumpled hat appeared; a few more, and a woe-begone face was disclosed; then a tattered shoulder; and gradually, as the sculptor, chip by chip, clears away the rough covering which surrounds the latent form of beauty in the marble block, so, sod by sod, the body, legs, and finally the whole form of Mr. Phelim Mc Gowan were brought into view.

Trembling and sheepish he creeps from his hiding-place amid the laughter of the unearthing party, and throwing himself on his knees before the priests, implores them to have mercy and forgive him.

At that moment, however, the mid-day *Angelus Domini* bell comes sounding from the chapel up the mountain side, calling all good Catholics to wonted prayer. Laughter ceases instantly, hats are doffed, heads bowed, and for a few moments, while the customary prayers are being rattled off and crossing accompaniments gone through, there is a lull.

"Bring him along, boys," says Father Maguire then, when their hats were on their heads once more, without vouchsafing Phelim any further attention; and he is led away, protesting dismally that he was always true, and that nothing would ever have induced him to vote contrary to the directions of his clergy.

The appearance of his son Terence soon after, at a sudden turn of the road, reduced him to a condition of most pitiable perplexity; and it was only by dint of the most ghostly threats and physical exhortations that he could be induced to adhere to his lately expressed political opinions.

When Terence discovered who it was that was struggling in the midst of the party, his indignation was unbounded. Father Maguire tried to bully and assert his spiritual authority, but Terence would neither be bullied nor admit his spiritual jurisdiction in his present temper of mind. He insisted upon his father's release, and, notwithstanding that he was only one against ten or more, made as though he would effect it by force. He was a powerful man; but of what use was one man's strength? The others were only waiting for the priests' word to beat him into a jelly. But their reverences were men of peace: the sacred character of their calling would not permit the sanction of violence; and he was referred, instead, to his father's own deliberate desire to go with them. Phelim was told to express that desire at once for his satisfaction, and complied with becoming obedience.

"Never go agen your clergy, Terence; it's your own father that tells ye that."

He was hustled on at the same time, and

Terence, making an attempt at rescue, received one on the head, which laid him senseless on the ground.

When he recovered consciousness he had the road to himself. The men of peace had gone upon their way rejoicing; and he staggered on until he reached his own cottage, where his broken head stirred up once more the subsiding agitation of his mother's heart. Oh, these elections—these elections!

If Terence had arrived before that fatal priestly visitation, his father would have been carried off to the fastnesses of Corranmore; now a more plausible fiction could be substituted, and Mrs. Mc Gowan had been keeping him carefully out of sight until he could get down with safety to the rest of the tenants, and none deplored more than herself his capture by the enemy.

As he returned that evening to Geraldscourt, sick and weary, under a lowering sky of murky clouds shot with fiery red, Terence was full of gloomy thoughts, and it was a relief to find that the influx of other voters from the estate, and the free circulation of whiskey, had removed, to some extent, the depression which prevailed in the morning.

Another crowded night, and a sleepless one for many in that house, and the election morning dawned. Cars innumerable came rattling in in quick succession to carry the voters to the poll, Kilmorris being a good ten miles and more away; there was a bustle of eager excitement throughout the premises; the dragoons were looking to their accoutrements, watering their horses, and making preparations for starting; and whiskey was still flowing to produce the courage requisite to face the anticipated dangers of ambush parties, intimidation, assault, violence, tumult, and riot. Breakfast has been distributed, the cars are n readiness, packed with full cargoes of trembling suffrages, the dragoons have mounted, and received Glenboy's word of command, whatever that may be, to dispose themselves at intervals on either side of the cavalcade, and they only await Rochfort's coming to make a start.

It was Nora who detained him; she was clinging to him and imploring him not to go.

"Indeed, indeed, papa, it's no foolish fancy, — grandmamma can tell you that it's not! Speak to him do, for Heaven's sake," she cried, turning to Lady Eleanor, "beseech him to stay away."

"No, Nora, it is his duty to be there; let him go, my child," said Lady Eleanor, firmly; though it was evident that the memory of that midnight cry still hung upon her hidden thoughts. After all perhaps it was not for him. And yet that hideous fevered dream of Nora's! Still, he must go: and he went.

Bartley Mc Loughlin, Pat Connor, Terence Mc Gowan, and a few other stalwart non-voters had been distributed among the cars to take care of their valuable freight, and form a body-guard when they arrived at Kilmorris; and when Alan had mounted his horse and joined Shirley, the procession started in a curious mixture of apprehension, laughter, and excitement; leaving many an anxious heart behind in mountain homes over which the white morning mists were still hanging, pierced here and there by shafts of silver sunlight.

Shortly after they had disappeared from the wondering view of the lodge-woman, they were joined by the Protestant clergyman of the parish, who, in right of his fat glebe lands, was going to exercise his privilege of voting for the ascendency of his church, and who was naturally very glad to avail himself of the escort which Rochfort had provided. His stout cob carried a very fair specimen of the Irish country parson who has been so unnecessarily belauded of late, and who, now that he is at the mercy of synodical laymen, will, perhaps, awake from his easy-going apathy, and find out that ministering Protestantism means something more than the profession of sound Orange principles. (5) He had, perhaps, fifty Protestants, all told, under his care, was exceedingly fond of fishing, proud of his education in Trinity College, Dublin, a powerful plagiarist of the strong Conservative views of his Dublin daily paper, a master of his country's brogue, and, like most of his kind, a bore—having no particular goodness of life, or zeal, or piety to set off against the intellectual deficiency with which Nature had endowed him, and the limited education and cultivation which he had undergone. There is no reason why we should be bored as well as Rochfort, so we may just canter on with Glenboy to the head of the line, which was already leaving the mountains behind, and dragging its motley length into the grassland plain which stretched away to Kilmorris, and beyond that again, many a mile away to Dublin.

The farther they went from the mountains the more decided became the change in the faces and appearance of the farmers and country people along the road. The picturesque variety of feature to be seen in the mountain districts wore gradually down as they neared the borders of the old Pale into a more monotonous and dogged English type: and to-day there was that upon the faces of most which portended no quiet victory for either side. They exchanged preoccupied and almost silent greetings; their sticks were clutched with a pregnant meaning; and throughout the thickening crowd there was discernible that shadow of ominous intent which marks the impending party-fight in Ireland. The deadly hatred which Ribbonmen and Orangemen—Protestant and Catholic—had been nursing against each other for weeks past, the fierce eagerness for revenge, the cruel lust for blood, and all the volcanic elements of the Irish nature—whose picturesque inequalities, like the fair landscapes of the earth, are but the surface-covering of violent and devastating fires—were gathered and concentrated into a gloomy silence like that which precedes the terrific bursting of a storm; and it was impossible to move along through them without feeling conscious of their influence. Even the rowdy fighting-men, with hay-bands round their legs, to whom a fight was the best entertainment you could offer, felt that it was no rollicking faction-fight they were going to take part in, but one which hate, and hate alone, was to direct, through the medium of that cursed party spirit which Orangemen bring their boasted brotherly and religious love to cherish, if not to keep alive altogether.

The long procession of Conservative voters was looked upon with no very friendly eyes as they passed; nor were the soldiers treated to any very demonstratively affectionate looks. But as there is a very wholesome respect for the British soldier in Irish country districts, and as the people have an unaccountable aversion to fire-arms in anybody's hands but their own, their ill-will at present went no farther than a muttered threat or two. Notwithstanding their escorts however, and the evident restraint which it caused in the hostile feeling along the road—notwithstanding, also, the presence of large bodies of policemen marching along in the same direction—Rochfort's cars were very silent and very trembling; and when, about a mile from Kilmorris, they were suddenly brought to a standstill, a general consternation immediately ensued. An orderly galloped rapidly to the rear with a message from Glenboy, and it ran down the line at once that they had been attacked. Some jumped off preparatory to flight, and the threats of Terence and his fellows would have been insufficient to restrain them and prevent a general rout, if Rochfort had not hurried up to reassure them. He didn't, however, make known the cause of the stoppage, which was a message from the magistrate in command of the troops in the town to the effect that, from information he had received, he had reason to believe that a party had been told off to lie in wait for this contingent, and that he had therefore despatched a company of infantry to strengthen their escort, for the arrival of which they had better wait before coming any further. For some minutes, therefore, they remained where they were, a prey to extraordinary fears, which were expressed with all the amusing gesticulatory play of countenance which makes an Irishman under the influence of any emotion so interesting an object for contemplation.

The infantry arrived, and were directed to receive the cars within their protecting lines (military readers will excuse the omission of the exact terms of the order), and with a file on either side of every car, in addition to the cavalry, they performed the remainder of the march in comparative and leisurely security. As they neared the hovels and the expensive stone buildings of poor-house and lunatic asylum which formed the entrance to Kilmorris, as to most Irish towns, the mob and sounds of riot and disturbance increased; the usual beggars of the dirty streets were merged in the struggling masses, which were shouting and menacing opponents up and down the one principal thoroughfare; and the flags and party emblems which flaunted amid the riot added another fluttering element of fear to the minds of the wretched voters, who were converging from different directions towards the court-house. The cross streets were filled with soldiers; policemen in large bodies were stationed at all the available vantage posts; and magistrates and officers were riding backwards and forwards in a flurry of nervous excitement, cheered or hooted, if not pelted, by the chaotic elements of riot amid which they forced their way. Already the streets had been cleared once, and the soldiers were not in the best of odour accordingly, and were receiving the stones, brickbats, and what-not with which they were favoured, with the unresisting dignity which their country requires of them on such occasions.

Poor Captain Hillier, who fortunately had not been left in charge of the troops, came bustling up to Rochfort, as his party wound their way through the yells and hooting and jeers of the surrounding mob, and gave him a most doleful account of their prospects. The Radical mob, he said, had entire possession of the town. Some Conservative voters who were to arrive by train, they had met at the station and shamefully maltreated, and it was supposed that two or three had been killed; even as he spoke they heard the word given to charge, and saw the brandished sticks and crumpled hats flying down the street before a troop of cavalry, who had been kept sitting quietly in their saddles for some minutes past amid a shower of missiles of every kind. The din was tremendous, deafening: cudgel play was going on at every corner. "Yer sowl to glory!" and similar accompanying apostrophes, being followed by resounding thwacks upon unguarded heads, which were rapidly developing abnormal bumps that would have puzzled a phrenologist as sorely as they did the recipients.

As Rochfort's party, strongly guarded, made their way towards the poll, a yell from the opposite direction announced the arrival of a party of the other side, and a wild mob, driving all before them, burst along the street as the advance guard of its Radical following, and despite the exertions of the soldiers, the scrimmage soon became general. It was the wildest scene conceivable. The frantic fury of the people had been roused to the utmost pitch by violent harangues from Father Maguire and other priests, who mixed personally with the mob, and led them on to secure the avenues to the polling-place.

There was a forest of sticks waving furiously over a motley floor of curses—wretches being trampled to death underneath, and knots of voters being torn hither and thither, amid the hurly-burly mad confusion, struggling with an abortive instinct of self-preservation, and experiencing to its full extent the dignity and delight of being the depositary of their country's franchise. At last the Riot Act was read; the soldiers received orders to load; charged again amid a volley of paving stones which emptied some of their saddles, and inflicted serious injuries on others, and yet they had no order given to fire or otherwise defend themselves. The magistrate in charge was afraid of the responsibility, and they were sacrificed accordingly without power of retaliation.

The street is temporarily cleared, and the mob, with a few unfortunate Conservative voters intermingled, but perhaps unknown, roared and yelled, and flung stones from a respectful distance. Rochfort polls the greater number of his votes, and from a window of the court-house, where he stood with Shirley, breathless from the late struggle, and looking down upon the scene with eager eyes, he sees a couple of his own voters being carried off down a bye-street to the lake, and in a moment is once more in the crowd, with Terence and Pat Connor hotly in pursuit.

Too late : they had put off from the shore before the pursuing party reached it, and were mockingly laughing as they pulled away across to a distant promontory.

"Quick Pat," cried Alan, "get a car from the hotel yard," and we'll slip away down along the shore, and be there before them. They'll not see us till they land. Quick now, or they'll beat us."

Away went Pat through the back alleys in the neighbourhood, and Rochfort and Terence stood watching the direction of the boat till he returned, with another boy or two, just to make sure, as he said.

Rattling through back streets, they soon left the tumult of the town behind, and made the old horse go as he never had gone before, until they came towards an open, from which the boat party might be seen. Still in the same direction, and a race, by Jove! And a race it was. "Now or never, Pat!" cried Alan, taking the whip, while Pat Connor worked the reins, and the rest encouraged the animal according to their kind; and as they turned the last corner they could see the abducting party hurrying off their victims to a car in waiting. It had been high pressure before, but now it was a question whether any reasonable wind of decrepit age could possibly stand the strain which was being put upon it. It was touch and go. They wouldn't, in all probability, have done it; but a fault of judgment of the other party saved them. Thinking they would be intercepted, they suddenly changed their tactics, and made for the boat again. The pursuing car was violently pulled up, the occupants sprang to the ground, and in a moment were in full pursuit across country. It was a race again : but the boat party were heavily weighted by unwilling feet, and Alan and Terence were already in the same field with them. They reach the boat, throw in their cargo, she grates along the shore, and in another moment they would have been out of reach. But alas! and alas! the weight was all at the stern, and her nose keeps banging against a rock; and while the hindmost man, who is pushing off, is breaking out in bitter curses, the others are upon him, and he is stretched his full length in the water at his feet.

Madly back, then, with their rescued votes to the town, where the tumult and turmoil of the streets had become intensified in their absence, by the discharge of a soldier's musket, which had killed a man among the mob. Human nature could not passively submit to the provocation these soldiers were subjected to, when the power of retaliation was in their hands; and no jury could ever find that man guilty of manslaughter for not waiting for the still-delayed command of his officer to fire. Still the result had been disastrous; for instead of expending their hate upon each other, both parties now had seemed to join their fury against the soldiers and magistrates and all the authorities who were connected with the outrage, as they deemed it. The pavements were ripped up, and the air was alive with broken fragments, while the houses on either side were ringing with the most blood-thirsty threats. Torn banners were waving above the crowd; processions had been swallowed up in the heaving sea of passion; and the election seemed to have been, for the time, forgotten. It was a chaos of indescribable turbulence and fury, wild, reckless violence and unmastered rage, such as Ireland only, under a strong Government, is capable of producing.

Happier for Rochfort and wiser would it have been if he had abstained from committing himself to the dangers of such a seething cauldron of infuriated madness. But the very danger fired him with double determination, and he plunged into the midst with his handful of followers, and made straight across for the court-house, regardless of the savage faces that opposed his progress with threatening cries and sticks. He caught a glimpse of Brady looking on with a triumphant smile upon his heated and repulsive features, and pressed on more eagerly than ever, determined that these votes should be recorded. His stick was of the toughest and the strongest, and there were few men who could wield it better than himself. The crowd gave way before the sweeping blows he dealt about him, and now that his blood was up, these blows were no light ones, and many a cudgel was shivered in its owner's hand, as it came in contact with the nervous vigour which Rochfort infused into his strength. He was ably seconded by Terence and Pat Connor, and the sight of a handful of determined men dealing destruction among their numbers, diverted for the moment the hostility of the mob from the soldiers, and they bore down upon the struggle in overpowering and yelling numbers. Rochfort became separated from his party: it was in vain Terence put forth all his strength to reach him again; the pressure of the crowd was irresistible, and he saw him with difficulty gain the pavement, and set his back against the wall, and, single-handed, keep the fury of the savages at bay. Pressing eagerly to the front was a red-headed ruffian, with a face all bruised and distorted with a fiendishly revengeful rage, whose shout of "Down with tyrant landlords!" "Death to all oppressors!" was amongst the loudest of the cries that rang around, and stirred the Ribbon instinct to its depths. Still Rochfort maintained his footing, and warded off the murderous blows which a dozen heavy sticks at once were aiming at his head; and if a brave man struggling with adversity is a sight for gods, a strong man fighting, as he was, against overpowering odds, is a spectacle for men which might have stirred a chivalrous thrill even in the savage breast. But fierce ungoverned rage and party hate knows not of chivalry, and for all the fire of Alan's spirited defence, a few moments more must inevitably have decided the unequal fight.

But stay! What's that? There's murder in that sudden sound. A pistol shot rings out above the shouting and the din, succeeded by a cry which wakens a subduing horror through even that deliriously raging host. Rochfort had fallen to the ground with the blood trickling from a bullet-hole in the middle of his forehead.

Quick as ordinary multitudes are to change, an Irish populace is quicker. The foremost of the crowd, who had a moment before been animated with the most bitter and blood-thirsty feelings against the fallen man, sprang back, horror-struck, upon their fellows when they saw how some hand unseen had baulked them of their prey. The flourished sticks were lowered in an instant, and a loud murmur of indignation ran through their ranks. They would have beaten or trampled him to death in the fair fight in which they had been engaged; but shooting for once appeared very near akin to murder, and when the news spread along the street there was an awed and guilty lull, amid which some of the most savage of his former foes picked up the prostrate body, and while others went before to clear a passage, conveyed it with all the gentleness they knew to the hotel across the way.

In a few moments Terence Mc Gowan and others of his adherents came breaking through the crowd, wild with grief and rage, and revenge suspended only till they heard the truth confirmed.

Terence meets Dan Nolan in his passage, with a fierce exultant look upon his face, and at once he knows, or thinks he knows, who fired that shot.

Shirley and others of the neighbouring residents are soon upon the spot, and one glance is sufficient to show them that Alan Rochfort's laugh would be heard no more among them.

The confirmation of the first report soon makes its way abroad, and brings about the fiercest conflict of the day. His tenants, with the tears running down their cheeks, burning for vengeance, wholly forgetful now of their own lives in their fury to avenge his death, burst out into the street from the place of safety where they had been lodged; and though no pistol had been found, and there was no apparent ground for suspecting Nolan any more than the other men who pressed upon him at the time, they caught up his name and sought him through the crowd like bloodhounds; bent upon scattering his brains upon the pavement if they should come across him. But he was no longer to be found, and they wreaked their vengeance instead on all others who opposed them. Many more joined in upon their side, and many of the other side to whom Rochfort had been well known, either personally or by favourable repute, slunk away home ashamed and sickened at the work they felt that they too had had a hand in.

The poll was closed, and Shirley was beaten; but he had no heart now to feel the disappointment, and the triumphant shouts of Brady's supporters broke meaninglessly on his ear. He took upon himself at once the control of all necessary arrangements for the removal to Geraldscourt; and an hour or two later, as Nora looked wistfully out at the trees waving weirdly in the darkness like giant funeral plumes, as her foreboding fancy suggested, a long and dark and sad procession, with blazing torches at its head, was moving out of the still riot-haunted town, and slowly leaving the shouts of triumph behind, as it wound along the road to Geraldscourt.

It was her father returning to his home.

CHAPTER III.

It is nothing to say that Alan Rochfort's death created a profound sensation over the whole country; any other magistrate or country gentleman meeting his end in a similar manner would have produced the same excited feeling of insecurity, and roused the same bitter comments upon the timidity and incapacity of a Government which professed to administrate, and which delegated its power to lawless ruffians under whose executive authority murder was no crime. In Rochfort's case, however, the sensation of horror and indignation was no stronger than the feeling of regret with which his violent end was almost universally regarded. There were few men in Ireland so well known as he; and Lady Eleanor had always been proud to think that her son, with all his faults, was the most popular man in the country. There was not a corner of the land where his generous hearty Irish character was not regretted; and about his own neighbourhood, and on his own estate, who shall describe the feelings with which the tidings of his death were received?

"We, ourselves," said the *Kilmorris Chronicle*, "were witnesses of the passionate sorrow which was felt by the unsophisticated mountaineers when the news was brought to them. They tore their hair, and beat their breasts, and filled the air with the wildest lamentations. 'Oh! God,' they cried, 'and is the darling fellow no more, that was the best friend that ever a poor man had? Is it gone from us he is entirely, in the pride of his life and the flower of his strength? we'll never see his like no more;' and we believe and fear they never will. A new class of landlords is coming into the country, who have no sympathy with the people; no hereditary claim upon their affections; who are saturated with the commercial spirit of the age, and who look upon property merely as a speculation; who have no respect for a poor man's feelings, and who are daily widening the breach which they have created between owners and occupiers in this unfortunate island. Such landlords as the late Mr. Rochfort was are beacon-lights among the shoals — beacon-lights of benevolence and generosity, and liberality, fairness, and impartiality, and whatever other virtues are contained in a just appreciation of the maxim that *noblesse oblige* — a maxim so thoroughly well understood and practised by the temporarily defeated candidate for the county; whose battle Mr. Rochfort so bravely fought, and whose triumphant return we confidently anticipate, when the proceedings at the late election shall have had that searching investigation which we are sure the unfortunate gentleman whose death we are recording would have been the first to demand."

We need hardly follow the Conservative editor any further in his panegyric on the public, private, and political virtues of his deceased subscriber; nor need we hear how the editor of the *Independent*, while regretting that the late Mr. Rochfort should have exposed himself as he did to the natural exasperation of the people, could not refuse to pay a tribute to his character as a gentleman of old hereditary standing in the county, as an impartial administrator of justice, and, above all, in his capacity of landlord!

The popularity which he had enjoyed among all classes, the respect which he had won for disinterested impartiality on the bench, and the gratitude which he had earned for the mistaken indulgence and liberality and sympathy which had always characterised his relations with his tenants, were fully demonstrated by the immense concourse of people of every grade who flocked to his funeral. It was said, and no doubt with truth, that such a sight had never been seen in the county before. From the hall-door at Geraldscourt, where the tenants were assembled in their mourning badges, all down the avenue, and along a mile and more of road between the place and the churchyard gate, there were lines and lines of carriages and cars; old men and women recipients of his bounty, and many of the reckless mob itself amidst which he had lost his life: not one of whom, in cooler moments, would have raised his hand against a man whose name had been so loved as his throughout the county. Bitter were the curses launched against the unknown assassin, and passionately wild and touching were the accents of grief which thrilled along the line as the waving plumes came into sight. The sternest heart could not have passed unmoved through that long, bursting, wild lament which broke from the deep idolizing love and gratitude of those simple peasants, whose warmth of feeling and devotion are as deep and strong and irrepressible as the wildest of their wild desires.

The last rites are over, the grave has closed for ever upon their murdered master, and the vast assembly is returning in broken groups along the dusky lanes. As a living reality he is clearly now no more, and what is to ensue? The apprehensive qualms of selfish interest, which had been restrained as long as he still remained above the ground, broke out now into open expression, and men began to speculate upon the future of the property. It was felt that the old *régime* was at an end; what the new would be, and who would hold the reins, was now matter of absorbing interest, sufficient to abstract them for a time from the recollection of the tragedy at the final scene of which they had so lately been assisting.

Around the fires in public-houses far and near that evening there were anxious groups collected, discussing every possible eventuality, and only agreeing that the change, whatever it might be, must inevitably put them in a worse position. At Geraldsbridge the post-office was filled with the neighbouring tenants and immediate dependants of the place, listening with eager interest to what Bartley thought upon the subject: and his thoughts were not reassuring. His late master had had very few secrets connected with the property which the bailiff had not shared; and without giving any precise reason, Bartley affirmed positively that the estate, in his opinion, would be sold. He declined to argue the matter: that was his opinion. Pat Connor ventured to dispute it, not willing to believe that his own services might possibly no longer be required, and not yet accustomed to the thought that an entire change of management might now be coming upon the place. Bartley, however, continued to fill his pipe without further comment, and the arrival of Terence Mc Gowan with news from the house put an end to the discussion for the present.

The will had been read, and it had oozed down into the servants' hall that, with the exception of a few legacies, everything had been left to his daughter, after all just claims upon the property had been satisfied.

"There's where it is," said Bartley, drily, as this proviso was communicated; and when further pressed, he at last informed them that when everything was paid there would scarcely be an acre left. How far the prospect was agreeable to himself his expression gave no clue; but it may safely be inferred that he contemplated it with no more inward equanimity than did the many tenants holding at will, whose equitable rights upon the land were in no way secured by law; who had paid large sums for the goodwill of their farms upon entering into possession, and who, in the event of such a man as Brady, for instance, buying up the property, could neither calculate upon prolonged possession, an acknowledgment of their claims upon eviction, nor a continuance of their present easy rent. They felt that the ties which for centuries had bound together landlord and tenant on that estate had been severed at a blow, that a troubled future was in store, and that they had no security to meet it with; and the prospect added a last element to the depression which they still retained from the saddening incidents of the day.

Terence, as he returned late along the mountain road that night, had other thoughts besides of immediate personal interest to occupy his mind, and increase the apprehensive fears of what a new order of things might bring to him as well as others. His father had never recovered from the fright the priests had given him, and the bleak cold heather-bed he had lain upon that night; for, doubting the continuance of their influence when not at his elbow, they had directed him to be taken into the mountains until the election was over, and he had been returned to his home more dead than alive. He had kept his bed ever since, and the doctor gave no hope of his recovery.

At his death Terence, having remained at home always with the old man, would enter upon his land according to the terms of his father's will; there being no lease, and the elder son, who was in America, having, therefore, no more claim to the reversion than any of the others. The will, of course, would be respected, according to custom, by the landlord; and if the poor master had been alive, Terence had no doubt but that, with this and the land he already held in his own hands, and the small farm adjoining which he had been promised, he should have been in a short time sufficiently well off to justify his appearing before old Thady O'Hara as a declared suitor for his daughter's hand. A rush of recollected love passed through him at the thought; but it was short-lived, for who could say what might happen now? Miss Nora, if she had her way, would help him in his suit, he knew right well; but Bartley had been so positive about those accumulated charges which were to rob them of her ownership that there seemed no hope of ever having her as mistress. He was still engrossed in a maze of possible contingencies, when on turning the last corner before the glimmer of his cottage came in view, his thoughts were arrested by a sound from that cottage door which startled him by the unexpected suddenness of its cause, and told him, in the wild Irish wail of grief, that his father was already dead.

CHAPTER IV.

BARTLEY Mc LOUGHLIN's surmises turned out to be correctly founded. Poor Rochfort himself could hardly have known the extent to which he had become entangled, in such utter confusion were all his accounts and papers found. The family solicitor, on the recommendation of the executors of his will, took up his residence for the time in the house, to try and reduce the chaos to some sort of order, and Lady Eleanor's clear head and business faculty proved invaluable to him in his difficult task. Creditors poured in on every side; mortgagees came trooping down with their several charges, and Lady Eleanor herself was astonished at the negligence and recklessness in money matters which she now found that she had only half understood.

Nora was still absorbed in the freshness of her

grief, not yet recovered from the physical prostration which followed upon the terrors of that election night, and the mere mention of her father's name would still bring a fresh silent flow of tears. She was only too content that her grandmother should manage everything as she might think best, and leave her to the free indulgence of her aching desolate thoughts; and Lady Eleanor, in the constant employment of business, and correspondence with executors and others, found a temporary forgetfulness herself; though now and then some word upon her page would, perhaps, be blurred and blotted by a falling tear.

She moved about that house of mourning with her old firm tread, in a stately dignity of sorrow which awed the hushed and frightened servants, who had not yet become accustomed to the black void they felt all through the house. The solicitor among his papers was conscious of a certain tremor as he heard her step approaching, and her suggestions were always received with a most becoming deference. Even Nora felt the influence of her stern self-command, and would dry her tears when she heard her coming—only to let them break out again afresh, perhaps, as she saw the upright figure by the fire quivering with suppressed emotion; or when, at rare moments, Lady Eleanor, too, would for a while forget herself to tears, and let her sorrow run its course.

So passed the days: men of business came and went; debts upon debts were added to the score; and it soon became evident that the greater part, if not the whole, of the property must go. Lady Eleanor had known all along that there could be no alternative, but she had forborne to hint as much to Nora; thinking that she had quite enough to bear at present, without adding grief to grief.

At last, she began one evening to break it to her gently, and was agreeably surprised to find that she had already contemplated it.

"I never could live here without him," she said, trying very hard to restrain her emotion. "And it's better the place should be sold altogether, and somebody come to live here, than to leave the poor people without any one to be kind to them."

"Well, I'm very glad you take it so," said Lady Eleanor. "I was afraid the breaking up of old ties and associations would have tried you a good deal. But you know, of course, my dear child, that you always have a home with me; and until you are married, I shall do my best to make it as comfortable for you as I can."

"I know — I know, grandmamma. You are are always very good and kind to me;" and the poor girl burst into tears again, and hid her face in her handkerchief. What thought of marriage could she have with the memory of her father's loss so fresh?

It was decided then definitively that the place and property were to be sold, and they must leave: that was a bitter thought, when it came to be really faced. But the preparations and arrangements incident to such a change were, at least, an occupation for the mind, however sad an occupation it was, wandering from room to room, selecting, discarding, lighting upon old memories of half-forgotten scenes and incidents; grief probed afresh at every turn by some slight object which recalled the buried dead.

Still it was an occupation; and it was not until the day before the really last, when the bustle and excitement of preparation began to settle down, that Nora felt what it was to be going to leave her home for ever. She was standing upon the terrace, where she had confessed another love a few short months before, taking a long farewell already of wood, and hill, and glen, where they had so often wandered in the shade of summer days gone by, and listened to the pebbly murmur of the stream, and caught the freshness of the summer scents upon the air. In all she seemed to find his life inwoven with her own, and now but half—a widowed half—remained, and that was soon to follow; and the overshadowed page be blotted out for ever. The river would flow on unheeding of the change; the purple heather bloom for other eyes; strange voices sound within the old grey walls, and echo through those deep-embosomed glades, where Gerald and herself had woven childhood flowers long ago, threading hand in hand with him the mazes of the hazel underwood. What cruel memories of gleeful days—of joyous picnics in those deep dells—of rambles over fern and green, through copse and brake, by river-side amid the clustering flowers, across the rugged sides of yon far hills,—what mocking cruel memories came crowding up to make the sense of loss more keen than ever, when it seemed that loss would be endured afresh, when all the scenes its presence haunted had been left behind! How long, she wondered, would it take the people to forget them! Not very long, she thought; when once their place was filled it would be as though they never had existed. A tear or two, a momentary short regret, and then their memory would die into the past, and old attachment would be forgotten in the new interest which would succeed. It was a saddening thought, and scarce did justice to the love of the warm Irish hearts around; who for many a long year to come would cherish a longing remembrance of the old family that was gone, eagerly inquire for intelligence concerning them, and pray with all the earnestness and ardour of their nature that every blessing might attend such of them as were left.

The last few days had been trying ones both

to Nora and to Lady Eleanor. The poor people, hearing that they were to leave so soon, had come flocking down from far and near to pray them not to go, or to get a last sight of them at least before they went. Every day there had been a weeping crowd before the door, and the simple pathos of their grief was as hard to face as the actual last farewell itself would be. Kathleen O'Hara had been up on this last day morning, broken-hearted at the prospect of never seeing her young mistress again; and, for all the improvement in Terence's prospects, she would admit no cause for joy when Nora was to leave them.

They would be sure to meet again, Nora said; and she made Kathleen promise to write to her when she was married, and tell her all about the people and herself; told her that she must always count upon her as a friend if ever she needed one, and gave her a locket as an earnest thereof and a remembrance of herself. Thus another parting was got over—there seemed to be no end to them, and her strength was almost exhausted before the real wrench of all had to be undergone.

The chariot was at the door at last—that old chariot that had seen so many years of the family: the luggage was packed, and Lady Eleanor was in the hall; but Nora was still standing at the drawing-room window looking out with swimming eyes upon the terrace and the river, and the woods and hills beyond. With a sigh that was half a choke she turned away at length, took one more look round the old room, joined her grandmother in the hall, and followed her in deep silent emotion towards the door.

The servants were standing about waiting to say good-bye, and as the two figures in their deep mourning came into sight, there rose from the motley assemblage of men, women, and children outside, such a loud wailing cry of sorrow, that Nora fairly broke down on the threshold. Lady Eleanor had to let fall her veil, and descended to the carriage with very little of her usual firmness of step; the maid-servants no longer try to hide their emotion, and even the men are obliged to draw their hands across their eyes, as with tears coursing down her cheeks, and failing steps, Nora sobs out her last parting words to the poor creatures who crowd about her, and cling to her dress with passionate distressing grief, as she tries to make her way through them to the carriage steps.

What a scene it was—this severing of the last roots of the old tree, that for long years had cast its protecting shade about the place—this rupture for ever and for aye of the tight-drawn ties of centuries—this passing into nothing of an ancient house, amid the loud-crying lamentations of its sorrowing people! The postilion's eyes are so dim he can hardly see to guide his horses through the crowd; they press round the carriage, sobbing, praying, crying—some eloquently silent—some passionately demonstrative—others clasping their hands, and raising their eyes to heaven with fervent gestures, struggling for one last look, one last shake of the hand; and following them with such eager longing tearful faces, that at last neither Lady Eleanor nor Nora could bear it any longer, and they sank back from the windows quite overcome.

It was the same thing at the lodge, and all along the road : the distressing sights and sounds of parting seemed never to be over ; at every cottage there were families waiting to give them their last blessing, going down upon their knees sometimes *en masse*, or throwing into most expressive looks and tones the forlorn and desolate acuteness of their conscious loss.

It was a progress of dramatic woe—another of those stirring scenes which are only to be witnessed among the passionate impulsive Irish peasantry, whose affectionate natures know no artificial restraint in the quick expression of their feelings; and it was not until long after the last cottage had been passed, and the last wave of the hand been given, that the objects of all this demonstrative grief recovered from the effect which it had produced upon them.

One after another, then, the mile-stones hurried past; the trees of Geraldscourt were hidden now from view, far away behind in the distance; the hard reality of Kilmorris began to break in upon their thoughts, and the view dissolved into the coming life beyond.

It was a busy day at Geraldscourt, however, when tears were dried, and silence had succeeded to the sad confusion of the morning. An auction was to take place next day; the inventories were not yet completed, and the auctioneer was to arrive that afternoon.

It was a strange collection of antique decay that the prying public of attorneys, and attorneys' wives, and neighbouring squireens were let in upon next morning. Old furniture of any date; old plate and pictures, and old court suits laid by in presses in old lumber rooms unused, which had a smell as of a rat or rats that had not tubbed for months; old everything, with very little else to charm the eye of Mrs. Brady and her followers, who gloat with a noisome glee upon the falling of a house to which, in the life-time of the owner, they never would have been admitted. The rapping of the auction hammer was music to her ears; it rang the knell of another of the old houses above her on the ladder. She liked to see the plebeian throng of cars before the door; called it a judgment on their pride; and wondered whether John had money in the bank enough to buy the old dismantled place. But for the petition which was coming on, she was sure he would have found the means somehow; and the thought of doing the fine lady in the neighbourhood, upon the ownership of those lofty rooms and ancient hangings, was passing sweet to dwell upon, whether it occurred or no.

For three days the sale continued, until not even a kitchen chair was left, and then the gaping multitude retired again; their purchases were carried off, and ticketed, perhaps—in memory at all events—with the ruin of the Rochfort race. The shutters were put up, the windows remained uncleaned, the garden was left to winter weeds, and until the Encumbered Estates' Court fulfilled its duty, Geraldscourt became a mouldering and empty shell.

CHAPTER V.

THE winter snows had melted off the mountain sides, the loughs among the hills were rippling to the breeze, and thorny brakes no longer creaked and rattled with encrusted frost. Spring had coaxed once more the lurking violet and primrose into view; the tender buds were bursting into freshest green, the birds were singing, and the air was soft; the mountain streams, so lately swelled with torrent snows, had run themselves away to tinkling rivulets, which chattered sweetly through the emerald fields, and plashed about the roots of twisted ferns, as they leaped and sparkled through the rocky wood, to join the river-reach below; wood-pigeons cooed upon the tall larch tops in the soft yellow evening calm, and watched their mates upon their nests amid the maze of green, or flitted over bluebell carpets through the wood. The air was laden with fresh scents, and trilling notes from little nests among the flowering may or tangled honeysuckle bowers; the trout were flashing in the stream, and tiny rabbits gambolling in the dell, and long-tailed lambs inquisitively staring from the limestone rocks along the hill. There was a joyous smiling calm upon the earth which is as delicious after violence and death as a bright blue morning after days of gloom and storm.

I hate a gappy and chasmatic style, but still I hold it truth 'tis better to have skipped and pleased, than never to have skipped at all. What pleasure could it be to trace the growing weeds at Geraldscourt; to sit from day to day and watch the unsuggestive shutters in their place; to follow the temporary agent in his vain attempt at lifting rents from off the property; to sneeze through dusty title-deeds; or—what indeed would have been even more to our purpose—chafe with Terence at the unreasonable pride of Kathleen's father, which now was the only obstacle to their marriage?

Before leaving, Nora had made Kathleen's interest

her care, and Terence now had land enough to make it no improvident presumption his asking to relieve her from her father's charge. Thady, however, had conceived a dislike for him in his period of comparative poverty, and was glad enough to have it now as an excuse to show his love for Kathleen by refusing. Kathleen, he said, was much too good for Terence; he had a better match in view for her, and his hard-earned money was not going to furnish a cabin such as Terence's. The Mc Gowans were good enough in their way, but the O'Haras had been accustomed to look higher, and as far as he had a voice in the matter, they would continue to do so, however unanswerable Mrs. O'Hara's arguments might be.

Kathleen being a good daughter, and fond of her doting old father, did not break into open rebellion at once, and scarcely listened to the wicked suggestions thrown out by her step-mother; who knew what *she* would have done if any love affair of hers had been so unjustifiably hindered. She met Terence as before, under the hawthorn in the dale, and in sequestered lovers' nooks; and their meetings were not a whit less stolen-sweet, or their love a shade less warm and constant and determined because papa had forbidden the banns. But when the spring time came, and the birds began to pair, and nature softly smiled upon the year with that subtle influence which swells through all her life at that gentle May-time season, warming the earth into a rose of love—then they did begin to feel, with some intensity, the harshness and unreasonable pride of the cruel parent bird, who so deferred their full and perfect bliss. And Terence, no less than Kathleen, began to revolve many things in his heart about this time.

It was a Sunday morning, softly, beautifully calm, with all a Sunday's still repose, the mountains dimly sleeping in a soft blue haze, and church and chapel bells the only sound which swelled upon the air, as Terence crossed the hill to mass; his thoughts divided between his love and rumours which had reached him on the night before of a strange visitor to Geraldscourt that day,—a visitor, an Englishman, they said, who came to view the landscape o'er, and purchase if he thought it fair.

The roads were all alive with groups and pairs,

and single men and single women, in their Sunday best, with shoes and cloaks, and blue frieze coats, and ribbons, and neatly knotted hair, all travelling chapelwards; and joining on to some of these who came from Geraldsbridge, Terence heard the latest and the most minute particulars of the recent arrival, who, it was supposed, was now at this moment at Ballyduff, if not at Geraldscourt. All were agreed that it was an Englishman, for had not his driver told them so? But there was a discrepancy in the reading of his name, some positively declaring that it was Marjory, and others equally clear that it was Banks, while Pat Connor pooh-poohed both sides and asserted that it was Marshby,—had he not seen the man, and what further evidence could be required?

A certain sum having been apportioned for the maintenance of the place until it should be sold, Pat Connor was still a walking gentleman, and as such entitled to lead the public opinion of the neighbourhood, until his ignorance of pheasant breeding should be established.

On the chapel green, among the groups which were gathered round the black wooden cross, erected in honour of the visit of the Holy Fathers, was Bartley the bailiff, an important, and for that reason, a more reserved man than usual this morning. He had been sent for to wait upon the stranger on the previous day, and therefore he stood now with his hands behind his back, a little oracle for each new comer to consult. They didn't get much out of him,—not much that was satisfactory at all events.

"He's one of them English chaps that wants to put every one to rights," Bartley said, with a tinge of dry contempt in his tone. "There's but the one way of doin' things in his opinion, and that's his own; and it'll be a very different way, I'll engage, to what some of yous on this estate is used to, if he's to be head landlord."

Bartley seemed to derive a certain quiet enjoyment from the momentary silence which succeeded his expression of opinion, and then some one suggested that if he was an Englishman the rents would be riz on them.

"I'll engage *you'll* not be gettin' your bit o' land for what you have it now, then," said Bartley, addressing the speaker. "You'll not be warmin' your shins at the fire all day no more, John Johnny."*

"That the poor master might be back with us again! God be merciful to him : that was the landlord, rest his soul! Damnation to the man that took his life, whoever he was!"

"This new chap likely 'll be learnin' us English ways of farmin'," said Terence.

"Maybe that," said Bartley; "by all appearance he knows every man's business better nor himself, no matter how long he's been born and bred in the country."

How far this latter observation may have been caused by an undercurrent of recollection on Bartley's part could not be investigated at the moment, for the priest was entering the gate, and every hat required the attention of its owner in salute.

Mr. and Mrs. O'Hara, with Kathleen and two or three attendant "boys" appeared a moment after, and the lily of Glen Annagh's May morning

* This individual was the son of one John Mc Cormick, always known as Johnny of that name, and was thus distinguished from other Johns Mc Cormick.

beauty eclipsed all other interests for the time. Conscious, yet unconscious, of the admiring eyes that were turned upon her, she had a pleasant, modest word for every greeting, and soon detected the form which, for the last few minutes, as she neared the gate, her heart had been fluttering in expectation of. Like an air from the sweet south Terence feels her presence breaking over him, and tries to check the feeling from finding full expression on his face; for the wags about him were playing off their humour in murmured jokes at his expense, and nudging him to be less backward in coming forward to let them see a proper lovers' meeting. He stands looking at her with a suppressed glow of conscious possession, until other less favoured acquaintances have had their say; and then, as their eyes meet, and he comes forward, what a lovely distracting blush that was which the boys around could claim no share in!

Mrs. O'Hara stops with pointed cordiality to talk to Terence, and Thady, with a dignified courtesy, bids him good-morrow, and goes on into the chapel. The rest follow shortly after, and the long rows of wooden benches are filled long before the priest had finished off the few confessions he had to attend to before reading mass. Beads are being handled meanwhile with great apparent devotion, and the sun gleams brightly in upon rude, gaudy altar decorations, ungainly pictures of the Virgin, and coloured cross-surmounted prints of stations round the walls, which may produce religious fervours in the rustic mind, but sadly offend a cultivated taste, however limited. There were many more looks and thoughts, however, in that congregation dwelling upon their sweethearts on this warm sunny morning, and enjoying in prospect the lazy afternoon of love beneath the shady hedges in the fields, or on the heather knolls, or by the river side among the blue forget-me-nots and flowers; and Father Hugh's conscientious delay in the confessional, and excellently long and moral sermon afterwards, were as irksome to the youth among his enforced audience as the prosings of a Protestant parson often are to the voluntary victims of his creed.

There was an unlucky wretch, too, who had

been found drunk on a holy day and was condemned to stand up with a white sheet round him during the whole service; and he didn't find the time pass too quickly either, his ridiculous discomfort being further prolonged after the sermon by the reading out of the names of those who had not subscribed to certain charities or funds connected with the chapel in which Father Hugh was interested, and who now heard their names proclaimed in public to refresh their memories. (6) Those who had not paid their dues, being obliged to kneel outside the door, escaped the reproachful glances of their friends at this point; and if they were wise, had most probably long before taken advantage of their position to escape away altogether.

The crowd came gossiping out at last—chatter, chatter, chatter; butter, eggs, and ailments; ailments, eggs, and butter—and breaking up into groups, wended their way through the cuckoo-haunted fields to their several homes to get their bit of dinner.

Terence stays behind for further discussion of the coming landlord, while Kathleen goes upon her way with joy-bells ringing in her heart at the prospect of that whispered meeting in the afternoon.

Not many hours after, when boys and girls were merrily gathering to their Sunday dance upon some customary spot, or uttering their low love-language under leafy shades, Terence might have been seen threading the appointed wood beside the loch, aglow with happy expectation; and ripe accordingly for disappointment when he woke the gentle echoes of the shore with Kathleen's name, and listening, heard no soft reply, but still the humming of the insect life upon the air, and the hollow, bell-like music of the water in the rocky chinks. A startled heron flapping from the water's edge was all the answer he received, and he watches it unconsciously sailing away into the dreamy air until it brings its lazy action to a perch upon a distant point of rock; then throws himself upon the mossy carpet, to wait and think and lose his soul in love and nature, as he looks abroad upon the soft blue shimmer of the day, the white clouds merging into summer haze upon the mountain brows, the fresh green islands sleeping in the perfect calm, the darkly wooded points, the glistening reeds, and the wild duck leading out her fluffy brood upon the still water, all unconscious of a man's proximity. The sound of far-off rowlocks and scarce-caught notes of music makes the silence and the solitude the more complete; and the old ruined castle on the dim hill-side, above the hanging crags, has a vague charm of other days about it in this lovely atmosphere, suggesting legendary lore of love and minstrelsy in pleasant harmony with lovers' thoughts.

And now his heart stops still a moment, as it hears a sound—a sound it may be of approaching steps—and he quickly turns, and hears a splash, and starts, and then subsides again as suddenly, as an otter's head appears along the shore, the precursor of a rippling line of silver light upon the water.

Happiness, some poet says, was born a twin; and there could be no full delight in nature, no complete absorption of the soul into her lovely hues, while a human want still pressed, and kept a constantly reminding check upon the sense. In every rustling leaf, in every dropping twig and sudden flight of bird, there was a quick recall of eager hope—a momentary fixed expectancy—too often disappointed, but expanding certainly into a thrill at last, intense and full, and flooding, like a rush of sunlight upon a darkened landscape, or the bursting of a rosebud into bloom.

Flitting between the trunks of the intervening trees appeared Kathleen's light elastic figure, approaching quickly nearer, and as he springs to meet her, nearer still, until emerging fully into view, their hearts run on before their hands, and meet at once and mingle in a tender, fond, embracing look.

It was a sweet seclusion by this lovely lonely shore, far out of reach of interrupting eyes or ears; and as they sat, this handsome, loving, simple peasant pair, feeding upon each other's words, and drinking in each other's thoughts through speaking eyes, your painter might have found romantic subject for his brush in these two foreground figures, and the green-vista'd, ferny wood, which sloped up from the loch far far away to the rocky heather-ground above. The fairies' green they called the glade in Irish, and little else but fairies passed that way; and Terence and Kathleen, as they sat upon its velvet moss, found no disturbing thought to mar the happy sense of being quite alone, away from all the world; alone with nature and themselves—themselves their world—and caring for no other life or interest beyond each others' whole absorbing sympathy of love. Terence would clasp his arm about her, and Kathleen's head would rest upon his shoulder, as she gazed up into his face with a depth of loving admiration, and bending over her, their eyes and lips would meet with a passionate and lingering intensity of love so full, so far too deep for words, that for long minutes the silence would remain unbroken, and they would forget existence in that delicious trance. And so amid such fond caresses, and low delightful lovers' talk, the hours flew by, the sun declined, the woods began to mellow in the evening light, and yet they stayed and paid no heed to time, such sweet forgetfulness was in that ecstasy of love.

It was the oft-told tale that never palled since Adam told it first to Eve in the rose-strewn bowers of Paradise; that breathes as freshly from above as ever, for all the motley garbs and various tongues, the changing manners, stilted chivalries, and mock proprieties in which, from time to time, it is arrayed; that tells us of a heavenly element which reconciles us to humanity, and that finds its simplest, best expression when divested of the nice conventionalites which Nature in her wilds abhors.

I don't, of course, mean to say that we can be all Nature in this civilized age. The extreme simplicity of attire which our early parents favoured has its advantages, no doubt; and if Eve had only behaved herself, such recurring nuisances as tailors' and milliners' bills would be unknown, and Mr. Poole, instead of constantly having heavy engagements to meet, would be, according to an exploded myth of childhood, a happy spirit in the air, lightly gambolling in space, instead of heavily driving in the Park. But whatever ladies may think and wish, apparently, to the contrary, so much nature is hardly desirable in the nineteenth century. *Est modus in rebus;* but a little mode may go a long way, and the less mode the more nature; and the nearer nature, with due regard to established propriety, the better—Q. E. D.; which brings us back to the calm-reflected islands, and the rosy-tinted rocks, and the purple twilight which is spreading o'er the scene; and we find that our lovers have taken advantage of our absence to give us the slip.

That does not, however, prevent us from knowing that before they rose to end that too short evening, the combined influence of lovely solitude and love, and Terence's persuasions, had overcome Kathleen's resolution, and she had consented to make what in the country they call a runaway match of their engagement. Terence was so wise and right always, he must be right now. Her father had no reason, no good reason, for keeping them apart. She loved him; but she loved Terence, she couldn't say how much, or how much more; and love of father, mother, brother, sisters, friends, are but like Brussels sprouts, offshoots from the one strong stem, which a lover or a husband represents. Terence, too, had said that if he had not thought she never could be wrong in acquiescing he never would have asked it; and, brave boy! she knew he would rather give up anything than bring her into any harm. And then to be his own, own wife!

And so the plan had been arranged and talked over with just a little tremor on Kathleen's part; but his strong face, as she looked up, smiling, when they parted, reassured her, and she turned with a buoyant step towards home.

CHAPTER VI.

RUNAWAY matches are very common among the Irish peasantry. The priests, as a rule, look after the morality of their flocks satisfactorily enough; but improvidence is not immoral, when it is made the means of additional support to the Church. It is more immoral and scandalous that the priest should not have his comforts, than that a family of paupers should be propagated for their own, their neighbours', and their landlord's inconvenience; and, therefore, the father who objects to his daughter marrying into a house where there is already one family living upon two cows' grass—or, even less, one pig's potato plot— is not generally encouraged in his opposition by the parish priest. Early marriages conduce to morality, and that, of course, is an overwhelming good to set against the infinite evils of increasing pauperism, upon which Dr. Malthus and his theories might with great advantage be let loose.

Such marriages are usually managed somewhat in this wise. The girl goes out for a stroll towards evening, very much as refractory young ladies in a higher social position have been known to do, meets her lover bold round the corner, embraces hurriedly, with perhaps a little nervous emotion, and thence they repair at once to the house of a relation who has consented to be a party to the transaction, and find several of the gentleman's friends assembled to drink the whiskey which he has provided, to wish the pair a great deal of happiness, and to enjoy an evening's merriment at their expense. The father, meanwhile, passes an anxious night, guesses what has occurred, regrets his obduracy, subdues his noble rage next day, and, putting the best face he can upon the matter, brings home the girl; gathers relations and friends that night to his own house for more merriment and whiskey, and gives his consent to the marriage, perforce, from the knowledge that his daughter's character would be compromised thenceforth in the event of his not doing so.

There are, of course, stern parents who resent implacably the outrage which has been done to their paternal authority, and refuse to have anything more to say to the truant child; and if Kathleen O'Hara had not had a very peremptory advocate in her stepmother, it is not at all improbable that old Thady would have sacrificed his love at the altar of his pride, and spoilt the enjoyment of her honeymoon. But it was so very clearly demonstrated to him that he would have nobody but himself on his own side, and that even though Father Hugh had set his face against runaway marriages, he would not get any support from him either in the present case, that he was obliged reluctantly to pocket his pride and take her back again to the paternal roof, and celebrate the event with the usual festivities. He paid off Terence, however, as he thought, by allowing him only half the fortune which he had given out in the neighbourhood that she was to have; but, even so, there was plenty to build a new house with. Terence already had the site laid out in his eye; and the day after he had brought Kathleen home to her mother-in-law's carefully washed and dressed embrace, they were sitting together by the stream along the birch-tree copse, talking over all their plans and prospects on the very spot where the new house was to be raised. It was not, however, to be commenced immediately. It was necessary to wait a little; to see what manner of man the new landlord would turn out to be, and what kind of management the estate was now to experience, and also what kind of security they were likely to have of continued possession. Terence was a little more provident than his fellows, and had set his heart upon a lease for his new house and the lands which he already held; hoping to add to them when opportunity offered and goodwill was to be sold, and then there would be no more feeling of insecurity to be feared if the property should change hands again.

There was a general and disagreeable suspense throughout the estate about this time. That happy condition of semi-feudal insolvency in which for so many years they had been plunged—a state of proprietorship in which all their sympathies and traditional attachments were bound up—a state so congenial to the casual nature of the tenant, and attracting him so powerfully towards his equally casual owner—was pretty sure to be at an end, and the necessity of paying rent occasionally to help a feudal, careless landlord was a lesser evil than what their hearts misgave them might now be in store. On one or two neighbouring properties they knew that regular payment was enforced; on Brady's, not a shilling of arrear was allowed, and notices to quit were served half-yearly, so as to keep a constant power of eviction hanging over every man. Might not similar management be in store for them? The most behindhand, however, had determined that they would not give up without a struggle, and encouraged each other to stand up for their rights, even before they knew that these assumed rights were to be invaded.

There was that, however, in the air of the new comer,—who was frequently seen now, and curiously inspected when he did occur,—which made even leaseholders feel a certain twinge of conscience in respect of violated covenants as to subdivision, and other minor infringements of their lease. He was a dapper, business-like little man, with a quick eye taking in all he saw, asking a great many questions, and talking with a clear, hard utterance; never smiling, and as different from their late landlord as steel from quicksilver. Barney had to drive him one day from Ballyduff to Kiltyfarnham, and even his facetious remarks provoked no appreciative laugh. It seemed as if he hadn't time to spare to laugh; and the Irishman's comic amplification of the answers which were required from him on general questions of local interest seemed to be looked upon as merely an impertinent and time-wasting ornamentation of the plain "Yes" and "No" which was desired.

Barney volunteered some items of information gratis occasionally.

"Do you see the tree there beside ye, your honour? That was the shockin' murder then was under that same tree. There's the mark of the poor gentleman's blood on the bark of it yet; and they're talkin' in the country that he'll be seen about the spot oftentimes, with a mighty big gash across the face of him. There's another bit of a hedge there beyant, where Sir John had a couple o' slugs put through his hat, holiday last was a twelvemonth ; and, indeed, that's the nearest ever they got to *him*, for all they're at him this good while back and forard."

"Oh!" said Mr. Marjoribanks; and there was a considerable pause.

"It's not much better nor a couple of months since the agent got a shot too," continued Barney, meditatively, as if pursuing some indifferent train of reflection, flicking up his horse carelessly at the same time.

"Shooting landlords and agents seems, by your account, to be a very common thing in this county, then?" said the Englishman, with some asperity.

"Well, it is, indeed," said Barney, cheerfully.

"You take it very coolly, at all events."

"Oh! it's a terrible country, your honour, and that's the truth."

Mr. Marjoribanks, however, was not to be deterred from what evidently, if properly handled, would be a profitable investment. Want of management he could see very clearly was the cause of the difficulties which he had heard were to be faced in dealing with Irish properties; and he would show his sceptical English friends what might be done by an energetic and business-like landlord, who knew what he was about. So the sale was concluded, and Mr. Marjoribanks became the purchaser, and was soon afterwards welcomed with acclamations by the assembled tenants at Geraldscourt.

He made them a little opening speech. The property, he said, had evidently been shamefully mismanaged. Justice was not done to the land. Their system of farming was bad. He should make it his business to teach them a proper system of farming. Much draining was required; works would at once be instituted. Then their holdings were too small altogether; this must be remedied. The farms must be consolidated and squared, and they must do away with open drains, and wasteful banks, and crooked ditches. It appeared that their late landlord had been a careless man of business; they must get into regular habits now, have stated rent days, and forget the slovenly ways into which they had been allowed to fall. He should leave nothing undone for the improvement of the estate;

they would always find him ready to listen to any suggestions in furtherance of that end, which was for their own benefit as much as his; and he had no doubt they should get on very well together, and that the most cordial relations would always exist between them.

Assembled tenantry regard each other in grateful silence. The new landlord was fresh from Lincolnshire, where all the tenants upon his property were tenants at will, and therefore he was quite in a position to understand the Geraldscourt estate, where the holdings were also almost entirely at will. He set about his work at once, and was utterly dumbfounded at the outset at the state of neglect and confusion which he found that he had to face. Poor Rochfort apparently had kept no books at all, and it was difficult to arrive at any detailed information whatever in regard to the various holdings : his memory had been very retentive, the bailiff said, and he had been accustomed to take rent on account, and in instalments just whenever or wherever they chose to offer it, and jot it down when he came home. Bartley himself, in fact, had been his principal book of reference, as of the late agent's, and it was to Bartley's mercy that the Englishman now found himself principally indebted.

"This will never do," he exclaimed, at last, one morning; "we must have a revaluation entirely, and have the rents adjusted to their proper value. I can see that the property is absurdly underlet: and we must get rid of half those dirty-looking cabins."

"Have you been long in this country, your honour?" asked Bartley, looking up drily from under his spectacles.

"Why do you ask, my good man? I've been quite long enough to see the evils of mismanagement; and I certainly shall not permit such a state of things as I find here to continue on any property belonging to me."

"There's some of them that sets great store by those same dirty cabins," Bartley said, indifferently, returning to his smoke-stained memoranda.

"I'm sorry to hear it; for it's quite impossible that they should remain. I daresay a good many will be required as labourers. That is another thing which must be set about immediately—a good row of labourers' cottages."

Bartley said nothing, but continued to pore over his papers, and his employer went on.

"Really, with so much to be done, it is not easy to know where to begin. I hear the river is regularly fished; that must be put a stop to at once. That man Connor, who I see lounging about, will do very well for a water-bailiff, I daresay; though he seems an idle-looking fellow. Have you found that list?—no; well, no matter. I'll write at once for a regular valuator, and every one shall be started on a new footing."

With that Mr. Marjoribanks sat down to his desk, and wrote to Dublin, to a land agency office, and requested them to recommend him a competent man, and to have him despatched by passenger train as soon as it was possible. He then took up his hat, and desiring Bartley to wait for his return, went out into the air to refresh himself a little, after all that inextricable mess of documents.

"Oh, yes; I've got my work cut out, I see,"

he soliloquized. "All that land there must be drained: there's a fine fall to the river: and I don't understand how it could ever have been left in such a condition. But, really, these Irish! Now I'm an Englishman, and, therefore, I understand how every thing ought to done; and I've been a landlord in England to no purpose if I haven't learnt some knowledge that will come in useful here. Land tenure is the same, of course, all over the three kingdoms. What is law in one is law in another; and however they may object to law in this country, they will have to submit to it under my rule. Here you, sir! what are you doing there with a gun under your arm?" This to Pat Connor, who more than once had brought himself into view in that costume, that it might be known what position he had held under the former owner.

"Lookin' for a rabbit, your honour, or any bit o' game I'd come across," replied Pat, feeling that his tail was not in that upright position which was usual with him. "I was sportsman to the late Mr. Rochfort."

"Looking for a rabbit, eh? Oh, well, you needn't trouble yourself to do that any more. If that gun is your own keep it at home. I shall have a regular keeper here soon, and then, I daresay, there will be some underkeeper's work for you to do. In the meantime, I think of making you a water-keeper, for I hear that every boy in the country is poaching the trout from the river."

"Oh, of course, your honour, I'll do whatever your honour pleases to tell me."

"Yes, yes—of course. Well, go home now, and when we get things into order a little, I'll see about your place."

So Pat went home to his wife, full of a growing affection for his new master, and the Englishman returned to his bailiff, and set out soon after on a further inspection of his recently acquired property.

The salutes of the country people he was too busily occupied in thinking and calculating to take much notice of: occasionally they met with a distant acknowledgment, but it didn't do to be familiar; they might be inclined to take advantage of anything of that sort.

Map in hand, he proceeded over each town-land with Bartley, who only furnished information when asked, and as each tenant came up to welcome him, he looked up from his map, with a "Well, sir; you are Michael Flynn—or Bryan Rogan—or Thomas somebody else—I suppose. A pretty state of weeds you have your land in. You ought to be ashamed of it."

"Oh, it's poor land, your honour,—the worst!"

"There's no land so bad but what may be improved by careful husbandry. The worse the land the more reason for keeping it free from weeds, and keeping what good it does contain from being taken from your crops. I must see better farming than this, if you are to continue in possession. But you have a lease, I see."

"I have, your honour. There's two lives left in it yet."

"Ah! and whose is this house here? I don't see any mention of another farm but yours hereabouts."

"That's a son o' mine that got married, your honour, and got a share o' the land."

"And were you at liberty to divide the farm?"

"Oh, the ould master never hindered a man that way."

"But are you not bound by your lease?"

"Well, may be that. But he's payin' rent now this five year on his own bottom, your honour, and it'll not be easy to put him out o' that now, I'm afeard."

"Is this the case, Mc Loughlin?"

"It is, your honour."

"I think, sir, you'll find it a very strange thing if this doesn't make you liable to ejectment," said the landlord. "A gross violation of your lease, and no notice taken of it! You don't suppose I'm going to believe that;" and he moved on, after making a note of the fact.

The tenant followed, giving Bartley a nudge, and saying—

"Well, your honour, when the master took the rent from him, it must be that he allowed him for to have the land."

As a matter of fact, the father in whose name the land was held, had hitherto paid the whole rent, and his son's sub-tenancy, though virtually recognized, had not yet become, by prescriptive admission, a separate holding; but it was a good opportunity for making it so now: and Bartley saw no reason why he should not do himself a good turn with the tenant by supporting his fiction. The landlord made no answer, but moved rapidly on.

"What is that cowbyre doing there in that potato plot—or is it a cowbyre?"

"It is not a cowbyre at all, your honour; but a house belongin' to a tenant o' my own."

"A tenant! What do you mean?"

"He's a cotter kind of a chap, your honour, that pays a bit o' rent for the wee garden."

The more the Englishman saw, the more he was astounded at the utter absence of control which apparently had distinguished the former management of the estate. Here was a hovel erected for the shelter of a nest of paupers, upon a rood of ground belonging to a farm held under a lease by which subletting was distinctly forbidden; and he would be more surprised still when he came to turn out the owners, to find that they were unwilling to go, and asserted a right to compensation for being ejected from what they were pleased to call their improvements. As it was now summer time, the family were not at home, and the house was shut up; they had gone upon their summer tour, and would not be back until it was time to dig the potatoes again.

Then again there were stretches of moorland covered with cabins innumerable, surrounded by patches of cultivation, which could not possibly provide adequate sustenance for a family. These must all be levelled: the land was only fit for sheep and cattle, and to sheep and cattle it must return. Split up into miserable potato gardens, it was impossible that any profit could be made out of it.

From one farm to another went the new landlord, laying out one sort of improvement after another, projecting draining works, importation of Scotch farmers, and, in some districts, wholesale clearances; calculating costs of cottage building, what returns this would bring in, and what outlay that would require, and sowing golden opinions among the various tenants he met, who were delighted with the genial sympathy he showed in all that concerned them, and looked forward to his proprietorship with quite an enthusiasm of regard. Then he returned to the still unfurnished house, had a very simple dinner, and spent the evening over parchment-deeds, plans, and letter writing; feeling what a field for his energy there was before him, and promising himself that he would teach the neighbouring proprietors, whose acquaintance he had not made as yet, how even an estate in Ireland might be turned to good account, if a thoroughly good English system of management was introduced.

CHAPTER VII.

VALUATORS, surveyors, bailiffs, and every other such engine of innovation and annoyance, for which an Irish tenant entertains an associated hatred, were turned on at once, with all their horrid accompaniments of books and pencils, and maps, and chains, and gaiters; and the property knew itself no more. At first, the unaccustomed nature of the proceeding struck the tenantry with a puzzled inaction, and they looked on like victims, scarcely appreciating the significance of it all. This temporary paralysis, however, lasted but a very short time. It soon became evident that measures for self-defence must be devised, and Bartley Mc Loughlin became more than ever in request; his virtue being frequently and severely tried by the offers which were made to induce him to misrepresent existing tenures to the new landlord. On the whole, he stood the test fairly well, when there was the slightest risk of detection, either by his employer, or by neighbours who would wish to employ his services in a similar manner; but having no particular cause to show favouritism to the landlord, whom he hardly knew as yet, in preference to the tenant, in whom he had a neighbourly interest of long standing, it was hardly to be expected that he should desert his class all at once in the interest of a stranger; who, for all he knew, might be a mere *bodagh*, an upstart of a fellow, who didn't come of the real race of gentlemen at all. He was accordingly very popular indeed at this time, and though he always persuaded the tenant, whose cause he was going to support, that he only did so support it because what he desired he had a right to claim; yet it did, nevertheless, get about that Bartley was not at all inclined to be hard on them with the new man, and that in most cases they might count upon him as a friend: the which belief multiplied by many the various statements and assertions and forgeries which were now daily flung at the Englishman, in anticipation of a coming rise in the rents of the estate.

Irish tenants, with the greatest respect for a "gentleman,"—a respect which probably they share with peasants of all countries,—regard him in his capacity of landlord as fair game for any deception which they may be fortunate enough to induce him to acquiesce in to their advantage, and think it only right to avail themselves of every opportunity which presents itself for discounting the hardships of rent-paying which they will have to continue to suffer at his hands, by bleeding him (under favourable conditions of acquiescence) as freely as they consider that they themselves hereafter will be bled. A landlord they feel to be a necessary evil, and obviously they owe it to themselves to minimize the evil, and make his sting as harmless as in their power lies, by whatever means a plausible invention may suggest for the purpose.

Therefore it was that Mr. Marjoribanks, the new possessor of the Geraldscourt estate, and an unknown Englishman too, found his office daily attended by innumerable applicants, for the fulfilment of innumerable promises which had been made to them for their advantage by their late landlord.

"Have you nothing in writing to support your statement?" he would ask.

"Oh! not a scrape of a pen at all I got; the ould master, God rest him! was not the man to break his word."

He had apparently been in the habit of promising leases promiscuously, and so far the promise appeared to have given all the satisfaction which the lease itself might have been expected to produce; for some of them, to have the greater effect, were dated many years back, and had only not been carried out because the promisee didn't like to trouble his honour too much. He had been liberal, too, in promising timber and building materials of all kinds; and some of the reclaimed lands, it had been expressly stipulated, were never to have a rent put upon them at all. He had allowed any tenant to sell the good-will of his farm for whatever he could get; and the new landlord could not believe his ears when one, who was giving up his land to go to America, told him that he had sold the good-will of his seven acres for a hundred and fifty pounds to a neighbour man, who was going to take the land.

"And what is the rent of your farm, pray?" asked the landlord.

"Six pound ten, your honour."

The questioner looked at him in utter astonishment. This custom of selling the good-will of farms had not been known in Lincolnshire; and when he first heard of it here, he couldn't understand at all how a tenant was to sell a right in his landlord's land. It was an economical anomaly, and must be stopped at once. This, however, was a *reductio ad absurdum* of the whole system.

That a man should pay a hundred and fifty pounds for the privilege of paying six pounds ten shillings a year was quite beyond his experience of land, and he couldn't of course permit the transaction: as if a man could possibly hold land at a profit, paying actually double the rent that it was worth? (7)

"And pray," he continued, after delivering himself of such sentiments, "do you consider that the choice of your successor rests with yourself alone;

that I am to agree to any one who chooses to make such a ridiculous arrangement with you?"

"Well, your honour, the old master never interfered in the like o' that at all: never said a word to any man, high or low."

"Now, sir, it's useless for you all to be coming to me and telling me what your late landlord used to do. He had his own way of managing the estate, and a very bad way it appears to have been. I am master now, and you will please to accustom yourselves to my ways for the future, and let me hear no more of what you used to do. I shall not think of countenancing the arrangement you propose. The farm must be given up to me, and I shall, no doubt, find a new tenant to take it, in the event of its not being thrown in with some of the adjoining ones."

"But, sure your honour's not going to hinder me from getting the price o' the land?" asked the outgoing tenant, aghast at such an unexpected invasion of a right which had been recognized by custom for years and years back.

"The price of the land! Of land that I have the

sole right and title to the possession of! Why, what do you mean?"

"I mean, your honour, that my father gave as much, and may be more, when he took the land, and that it 'll be a hard case if his own son's to be hindered from gettin' that back when he goes to give it up again: an' it the custom in the country this hundred years back and more."

"Well, all I can say is, that it is quite the strangest and most unreasonable of the many strange and unreasonable things I have seen since I came to Ireland. Go and send McLoughlin to me. I must enquire further into this."

When Mr. Marjoribanks—perplexed, unhappy gentleman—came to carry out his schemes for consolidating and squaring farms, he would be still more surprised to find that, whereas, he had thought himself possessed absolutely of the land which he had purchased, there were attaching to almost every farm which he proposed to take up, rights of a similar unreasonable nature, which at the peril of his life, if not of his equitable conscience, he was bound to respect and compensate: in fact, the more he saw of his property the more his high-handed confidence in his own knowledge toned down before the discrepancies of tenure which would not be overlooked, and which he was warned unmistakeably that he had better not disregard.

To him next came Terence, one morning, with a proposition for erecting a new house for himself.

"Have you a lease?"

"No, your honour, not at the present time, I have not. But I was a mind to ask whether your honour would be willing to give me one?"

"And did you propose building without one?"

"I did, of course, your honour: why not?"

"And why are you anxious to build yourself? Isn't it usual for the landlord to do that?"

"Not on this estate, your honour, it is not; nor never was to my knowledge. Mr. Rochfort was a very kind man, indeed, and would help a poor tenant greatly with timber and the like o' that; but the buildin' itself and all the improvements was done by the tenants all entirely."

"So it appears; and that's another way of doing

things that is very new to me." Mr. Marjoribanks, in fact, was beginning to find that land in Ireland and land in Lincolnshire were not managed so precisely on the same reasonable principles, which he had thought must be common to both. He was beginning to find that land tenure in Ireland was not at all the simple thing it was in Lincolnshire and England; that it was a complicated subject, very different to what he had been accustomed to, and one which, it might reasonably be supposed, was hardly to be mastered in the six weeks' gallop of a journalistic or pamphleteering tourist.

"But what security have you for the enjoyment of your house when built," he continued, "if you have no lease?"

"Little enough then," said Terence; "and only that a man 'll have some sort o' confidence in his landlord, it'd go hard with him surely to be turned out, and get no compensation. But there never was a man treated that way on this estate."

"It's a bad principle altogether, tenants making their own improvements; though with the absurd number of small holdings that I find on the property, it is not easy to see how any landlord could keep every man's house in repair. We shall change all that presently and have nothing but large farms; then it will be another matter altogether. That, however, will take time, I dare say; and if you are bent upon building you must have a lease."

" Thank your honour."

" Is this man a good tenant, Mr. Loughlin ? "

" He is, then, a right good tenant. There's not a more industrious or regular man on the estate," said Bartley; and Terence modestly awaited the result.

"In the townland of Stradryan, you say your house is," said the landlord, apparently consulting some map or book of reference.

" There's a few acres of mossland about Rath-na-modra, your honour, that I had a mind to reclaim one o' these days; the rest of it's all in Stradryan."

" Hm—Phelim Mc Gowan was your father, I suppose ? "

" He was, your honour."

" I see, according to Mr. Hodge's valuation, you are very much under rented. I should say that you will have to pay a third more, probably, than what you do now, when I come to readjust the rental."

Terence's countenance fell several degrees.

"Whatever good's in the land at all, your honour," he exclaimed, "it's myself that put it there these few years back; and though, of course, your honour may do with me as you like, it'll be a great hardship if I be to pay rent now for the labour I put into the ground."

The landlord was engaged at the moment in puzzling over the existence of Larry Mc Gowan as a tenant, and hardly heard the last observation.

"Who is Larry Mc Gowan?" he asked. "He seems to be mixed up in some way with Phelim Mc Gowan."

"He's a brother of mine, your honour, that got some small share of the land when he married awhile agone."

"Another subdivision, I suppose. Upon my word, I think your late landlord must have been mad."

"Indeed, he was a very good gentleman and a very kind landlord," said Terence, with a subdued impulse of regret, which Bartley, standing by, acquiesced in.

"If it was a kindness to let you do exactly as you like, and marry and settle upon a rood of ground that it was impossible to get a living from, then I can agree with you; but I must confess, I don't."

"This land was held at will, I see," continued Mr. Marjoribanks, reflectively bending over his documents, "and, therefore, there will be no trouble about arranging matters in this case. Your brother, of course, will have to give back the land."

"That'll come hard upon him, too," said Terence, "for he paid dear for it, and got nothin' but hardship from it neither, ever since he come by it."

"With regard to your lease, that will be arranged presently. I see there will be even more than I thought of increased rent; you are not paying up to half the present Government valuation!"

"If your honour puts that rise on me, it'll not be much use to me gettin' a lease at all, for I'll not be able to pay it; let alone the discouragement to a man gettin' nothin' but a bigger rent for all his labour. The old master would never have behaved by me that way."

"What the old master might or might not have done is perfectly immaterial to me, Mc Gowan. I take the property as I find it, and every man will be rented according to the value of his land. If you think the rent too high, you are quite at liberty to give up your farm, and I have no doubt there are others who will be glad to take it. In fact, it was this moment only I was thinking whether it would not be better that James Duffy, who adjoins you, should (consulting the map) take the whole of that strip up as far as the heather. There's not more than enough for one comfortable farm, and only that you talked of building, and seemed to be an industrious man, I should have had no hesitation in arranging it so. If I hear any more complaints, that is how it shall be; so mind that."

Terence was too completely confounded at this new way of handling tenants to make any reply for the moment, and the next in waiting was called up.

The man approached somewhat delicately; he

had a written agreement to present for the renewal of his lease, which was just expiring. The agreement was forged, like many others which had been already presented, and Bartley Mc Loughlin knew very well that it was; but it was no business of his to say so, when asked if that was Mr. Rochfort's signature.

It was very like it any way, he said; but declined to commit himself to a positive opinion upon the subject, not having seen him write it.

There were particular circumstances, however, in this case which made the landlord look again and again at the signature, and then at the man presenting it, and then at other documents of a similar nature, and signatures of leases in a drawer at hand. He asked a great many questions, looking uncomfortably straight into the man's face the while, but getting no change out of the Irishman's assurance, and eventually giving it back to him with an incredulous promise that the matter should be looked into.

Terence, meanwhile, after conferring in muttered bewilderment with others who were standing about waiting their turn to prefer some untenable claim, struck off home again, with a curious mixture of indignation, astonishment, and apprehension occupying his thoughts as he went. Even the younger Brady who passed him upon the road, with the scowl which ever since their memorable meeting in the wood he had treated him to when they chanced to meet, created but a momentary diversion in the current of that uncomfortable feeling of insecurity which he had brought away with him. This new man seemed to think that they were to be moved about just like pins upon a board; that they were of no more consequence than so many bits of stick or stone. It was a dangerous game to play, he could tell him that; and it was not the neighbourhood to play it in. This property had always borne the best of characters; but then why was it so? because they had always had the best of landlords. This new English fashion wouldn't do here, Terence was convinced, as he for a moment pictured himself turned out upon the road with his sweet Kathleen in her present condition. There came an unnatural look into his eyes at the thought; but it faded quickly back again into the mild light of love as he thought of her waiting for him now, looking out perhaps from the door, or thinking of him as she bustled about her little kitchen, which presented such a very different aspect since the retirement of his mother from the housekeeping department.

Then he thought of Larry and his prospects, and feared that he would not go quietly out; and if he was made to take his land, could he do it? and yet, if he refused—oh! if he only had a lease, like one or two fortunate men among his neighbours, who could snap their fingers for the present at the changes which they saw impending all around them. If his rent was raised, as threatened, should he take the lease and make up his mind to the loss of all the labour which was only now bringing in a profit? Ejectment was the alternative proposed—could it be possible that the man was in earnest? what would Kathleen say if all their plans were thus scattered to the winds, and they were obliged to leave the old spot, which even she had an affection for now as his early home? He wouldn't tell her anything about it. The cloud would blow over, and they would be happy as heretofore; and in the erection of that new castle in the air and the life which it was to enclose, all cares and temporary depressions were, for the time, forgotten.

CHAPTER VIII.

It is an ill wind that blows nobody any good, as the younger Mr. Brady had much pleasure in acknowledging to the fortunate air which had wafted Mr. Marjoribanks to Geraldscourt. The new landlord, it was said, was spoiling the whole country with law. Processes and actions of every kind kept the sheriff's officers in perpetual motion, and Mr. Brady, Jun. in perpetual employment on the tenants' behalf. He had won two or three cases for them against the landlord, and his barometer, accordingly, had gone up immediately to "set fair," and had remained there ever since. He had almost more than he could do. There were daily, almost hourly applications at his office, by one or other of the Geraldscourt tenantry, to take up or to make cases for them; and, winning or losing, he was generally able to accommodate them.

Mr. Marjoribanks was determined that they should see that law was meant to be enforced, and that the conditions which he imposed were not to be disregarded with impunity. Bartley had a difficult task now to keep in with both sides, and had already laid himself open to suspicions of leniency, at variance with the regulations to be enforced. Ejectment cases multiplied every day—some for breach of covenants, which were of course given against the landlord by a jury of tenants; some to regain possession of farms of which the leases had expired, but which the present holders preferred to retain, until they were forcibly dispossessed; others, to get rid of houses which never ought to have been built, but which the occupiers persistently refused to leave. In fact, hardly a man gave up possession without calling in Brady, to see if he couldn't do something for him. It was war to the knife all over the estate; the office was daily beset by complaints and objections and pleas of poverty, and a long family, and loss of cows and stock, and claims which refused to be satisfied, which were vehemently argued out before the landlord, and followed up by muttered threats, as both parties retired dissatisfied. Crops were being seized, and stock driven off to the pound; wholesale evictions were taking place, and the village was continually now the scene of impassioned partings between emigrants who had been bought out and had their passages paid to America, and the neighbours who had collected to see them off, as they do round a deathbed for a parting soul. Notices of increased rent, and rent for land which had never paid rent before, had been served all round, and the gale was coming due.

Many had declared emphatically that they would never pay : *spargere ambiguas voces ;* friendly warnings were given to the Englishman by neighbouring proprietors ; the men whom he had dispossessed and put into his labourers' cottages, struck work ; his roads were torn up ; his draining tiles carried off in the night; sullen looks met him on every side ; he even took to carrying a revolver : but still he persevered. Ribbonism had revived, or developed upon the estate. On dark nights, parties of men bound on unknown errands might be met upon lonely mountain roads. Dan Nolan was frequently to be seen about the neighbourhood now ; the suspicion of being their late landlord's murderer having merged into a new and terrible interest, which they found in him as a prominent Ribbon leader. Larry McGowan had been heard to say, that murder was only fair retaliation upon the landlord crew who turned poor families out upon the road to die; and, despite of Terence's remonstrances, was now a determined Ribbonman. The increase of poor rates, produced by the turning out of whole families who had no choice but to go into the poorhouse, was a cause of murmuring to all, and an expense to the landlord which was hardly compensated for by the levelling of their cabins and the recovery of their bits of land. Rebellion was spreading over the whole estate. Bartley McLoughlin was afraid to ride home at night now; process-servers were beaten; inoffensive and peaceably disposed tenants were "noticed" by armed ruffians to pay the increased rent at their peril. Mr. Marjoribanks had received preliminary warnings, which made him go about now with policemen always in attendance. But though he saw—only that he wouldn't see—daily evidence of the failure of his boasted management, he doggedly persisted; had the laurels cut away from about the door and approaches to the house; and on the very morning when he was to collect the half year's rent, received a letter from one "Will Midnight," preparing him for death that day if he persisted in demanding the increased rent, and accompanying the warning with emblematic signs of a coffin in deep black ink, a rude sketch of a man standing over it with another pointing a gun at him, and a drop of blood below.

Ribbon notices had been posted on the adjoining chapels on the previous Sunday, warning the tenants to offer no more than their former rent, denouncing English oppressors, and vowing speedy death to exterminators: and for all Father Hugh's remonstrances from the altar, and denunciation of secret societies and party work, it was evident that the mandate had gone forth, and that the Englishman's murderer had received his orders.

Still, he was not dismayed. Secure and comfortable he could hardly feel. But his confidence in the efficacy of a bold front and determined assertion of his rights was great, and he had an Englishman's pluck, and wouldn't be beaten if he could help it; and therefore he took his seat at the table in the office on this rent-day morning, a shade paler, perhaps, but otherwise as firm and collected as usual. The policemen remained on either side of his chair, and Bartley Mc Loughlin and the other bailiff in the neighbourhood.

The tenants, who had been talking together in groups outside, press into the room with no very friendly or reassuring looks; and the business of receiving money, deducting poor rates, and giving receipts begins. You'd know by them, as they say, that there was something in the wind. In place of the jokes at the expense of their poverty, or of each other, with which the paying of rent is usually enlivened, they handed in their dirty pound-notes with a sullen, silent air; and without comment from the landlord, who merely referred to the bailiff to know if the amount was correct, and then signed and handed over the receipt.

For a time all went on smoothly enough; the leaseholders, and what few had had no increase to pay, seemed to have been put forward first. Then there was a movement at the lower end of the room, succeeded by an expectant silence, as a dogged-looking fellow comes forward, fumbling in his pocket for his money-bag. This was one whose rent had been raised, as the landlord knew when he heard his name; and he felt that the storm was about to break. There was a significance in the man's manner which was not to be mistaken; and the hushed stillness behind him, and the increased crowd of heads at the doorway, were in themselves sufficient signs that something of exceptional interest was taking place.

He was a long time getting out his money, and the delay was rather trying. At length, after deliberately counting over what he meant to pay, he laid it down without a word upon the table —the old rent.

Bartley counted it, and announced the sum to his employer, watching curiously to see what he would do.

"You are 2*l*. 5*s*. short," he said, sternly, without a symptom of flinching.

"That's all the rent ever I paid before," said

the tenant, putting his hands into his breeches pockets, "and that's all the rent I mean to pay to-day; so make the most of it."

"You were regularly noticed that you had to pay an increase for the half year now expired. If you preferred to leave the land, you were at liberty to do so. You have not done so, and you must therefore pay the rent."

"An' if I was noticed," exclaimed the man, fiercely, "is it payin' rent I'll be now for what myself and my own family wrought at these years back to make it give a crop at all, when the land was no better than a bit of the bare moor, so it wasn't; and wasn't worth a shilling to buy out of face, except for the labour it got: that I gave it myself, and that I'd be to be payin' rent for now. But I'll not be doin' it at all. There's all the rent the late man allowed me for to pay; and ye may give me a receipt in full for that, or may be it'll be the worse for them as doesn't."

"I shall not take a sixpence under the full rent; and you know the alternative—a notice to quit will be served upon you forthwith if ——

The sentence was never finished. At that moment a man stepped out of the crowd, presented a pistol at the landlord as he sat, and fired. The report rang through the room, and a shout arose outside as Larry Mc Gowan burst through the doorway, which was cleared for his passage, and a moment after was speeding away towards the covert.

The policemen, taken aback for a moment only by the suddenness of the movement, sprang forward at the shot; but the doorway was not cleared for them; and before they were outside the murderer had disappeared among the trees. No one knew at first which way he had gone, but at last one man was reluctantly persuaded to indicate the opposite direction, and they hurried off at once upon the chase.

Naturally a scene of great excitement ensued about the office door. Mr. Marjoribanks was carried out by the two bailiffs lifeless, apparently; many looking on exultingly at the sight, and many more horrified in their hearts, but not daring to show any sign of sympathy in their faces. (8) The servants assembled in consternation, messengers were despatched for magistrates and doctors; and when the latter arrived it was announced, to the disappointment, perhaps, of some, that the ball had not touched the heart, and that recovery was not impossible.

Intelligence of the attempted murder soon flies through the neighbourhood, arousing mixed sensations in every hearer, and reaches Terence and Kathleen looking on at the erection of their new house.

Strange to say, Kathleen's, and even Terence's, first feeling almost was one of relief. As the news was told to them, the landlord was dead, and therefore there would be no rent to be paid the next day; when otherwise Terence and the rest of the tenants from that side would have had to attend. On the head of this rent poor Kathleen had passed miserable days of apprehensive fears lately. Terence had consented to the increase in consideration of the promised lease, making up his mind to bear the injustice with a good grace when there was no escape from it, and determining to set about reclaiming as soon as ever the house was finished, so as to make up by increasing profits, secured for twenty-one years, for what loss he considered that he had been made to suffer for his former industry. Take it as it stood, the land was not highly rented, and they might do well yet with energy and perseverance. Kathleen applauded the peaceable resolution which her more submissive spirit had been mainly instrumental in producing; and though they had not yet got their lease, the foundations of the house had been laid, and the walls were rising rapidly into a future of happiness and prosperity and comfort and joy in each other, and the little creature she carried in her arms— holding him up to Terence occasionally for admiration, and watching him as he nursed it and talked to it with all the tenderness and endearment of a woman.

But then another difficulty arose, more perplexing, more frightful than the last. Ribbon intimidation was rampant on the estate. Terence had always refused to be a party man, and continued to speak against the business now in a way that no other man would have dared to do so openly; and which, it was more than once intimated to him anonymously, would get him into trouble if he didn't take care what he was about. It was well known that his rent, among others, had been raised, and that he had been on the verge of eviction for objecting. It also became known that he had determined to accept a lease at the increased rent, and his submission was considered cowardly, if not traitorous, to his neighbours.

There were many of the wilder lads of the neighbourhood who bore him no affection, for he undoubtedly was overbearing sometimes in his manner, and made them feel their own inferiority too unpleasantly; and when the Ribbon Lodge decided that the increase was to be resisted, they were glad in their hearts at the prospect of obliging Terence Mc Gowan to surrender his will to theirs. No one, they well knew, disobeyed an order from the Brotherhood, if he set any value upon his life; and Terence, for the sake of his wife and child, would have to submit. So a couple of them had watched him away from home, and had presented themselves, with pistols and blackened faces, before Kathleen and his mother one afternoon, informing her that if the landlord's demands were acceded to he would hear from them again. Kathleen only recovered from the fright to lapse into despair. There was eviction on the one side, and on the other—what hideous stories had she not heard of Ribbon vengeance, where neither man, woman, nor child were spared, houses often burnt over their heads, and atrocities that made her shudder to think of committed without remorse! That hideous massacre at Wild Goose Lodge which she had heard her father talk of, when a whole family were burnt to cinders in the flames of their own house in the dead of night, was only one of the horrible tales which crowded up to suggest similar not impossible consequences from Terence's disregard of the intimation which had been conveyed. His own life, at least, never would be safe, and every time he left the house she would be occupying the time in picturing all sorts of horrors until he should return again. He was so proud and so independent, he never would give way to them; and yet, for her sake, perhaps he might. But then, again, if he did, eviction must be faced as the alternative. All her happiness was destroyed now, and Terence had no way of raising it up again when he was told the cause of the low spirits in which he found her on his return. If he alone had been concerned, he would not have hesitated a moment in braving the cowardly assassins, the secret terror of whose power, nevertheless, he was far from being indifferent to. An open enemy is one thing, but the bravest man may shrink from an unseen danger, which may take him at any moment unawares and defenceless. Still, he would have asserted his independence in spite of them if it had not been for his wife and child; and he pressed her to his heart in an agony of indignant love, as she sobbed out her fears upon his breast, and wished they were far away from the neighbourhood, where such torturing anxieties would not interfere with the happiness of their lives.

"I wouldn't like to leave the old place, Kathleen. A man has a great fondness for the spot he's been bred and born in," Terence said sadly. "But it's better go nor see you in this way, my own darlin' wife, that I thought I'd have made as content and as happy as the flowers o' May. And now all this trouble to come upon us."

"Do you think, Terence dear, if I was to write Miss Nora word? She told me that we'd never want a friend while she was living."

"There's not one I'd be beholden to before herself, Kathleen. But sure she couldn't help us now, mavourneen; not a much use writin' to tell *her* of these blackguard fellows what they're up to."

Kathleen felt that her best card had been played to no purpose, and they were both silent for some minutes.

"I'll tell you what you'll do," she said at last; "let them have their own way, and make believe to pay only the old rent, and I'll take the rest of it myself to the master, and ask him to not let on at all that ever it was paid."

Terence shook his head doubtfully. Such cowardly deception went sadly against his self-respect. Besides, they must take their lease at that same rent, and it would only be deferring the evil day.

Something, however, might happen between that time and rent day, and there was a ray of hope in the thought. There was plenty of time any way to think of it, and as he didn't go down till the second day he would hear how the resistance had gone, and then they could talk about it again. So he persuaded Kathleen to try and forget all about it until then; but he could see every day how it preyed upon her mind, and it only made him chafe more fiercely than ever at the utter impotence he felt between this Scylla and Charybdis of tyrant landlords and tyrant neighbours.

Thus it was that still perplexed, not knowing how to escape destruction from one side or the other, his mind not yet made up, waiting in suspense for tidings from below, the news of the landlord's murder seemed to take a load from off his thoughts. Hope would take care of the future; for the present he was free, and when he heard who the murderer was, the natural horror and shame which he felt at finding that it was his own brother was unconsciously lessened very considerably by the feeling of thankfulness at being thus relieved from a pressing and absorbing anxiety.

Murder and attempts to murder, under whatever counteracting circumstances of familiarity or pressure of other engrossing interests, must produce a certain thrill of sudden horror at the first announcement of their perpetration close beside us, and Kathleen shrunk back to Terence's side in a kind of awe at the termination which their troubles had found. She knew, too, how he would feel his brother's guilt, and looked up at him with a silent sympathy, as he inquired quickly for particulars.

"That boy, I knew, would never come to any good," he said, at length, with emphatic sternness. "Didn't I warn him often and often against havin' any concern with that Nolan and his comrades, and now he's damned his soul in this world and the next, and brought shame and disgrace on all his kin! Isn't it shockin' for a man to go take away life when he can't give it, let him be ever so hardly used? and not a doubt but the poor fellow was badly treated enough—that I'll never deny—but for all that, I never thought to see the day that any o' *my* name 'ud come by their death on the gallows. It's ill cursin' a man that'll do no more harm in this world, but it was a bad day for this district when that gentleman that's lyin' there came into it, and that's the truth. Trouble upon trouble, and blood now to crown all. Oh! Larry, why wouldn't you listen to me, lad, when I told ye what that idle sort of life 'ud come to? Poor lad—poor lad! Come Kathleen, let us get into the house and hide our faces from the day: not yours, acushla, but mine and his mother's there, that never should have seen this day. God forgive him for it."

CHAPTER IX.

"Well, I must say I think he deserved all he got," said Sir John Hillier, discussing the event of the week at Carrickamore Petty Sessions a few days after. "Heaven knows they're not too fond of me for the order I make 'em keep. But I'm hanged if I can understand how they kept off him as long as they did. Why, he was turning out every blessed sinner on the estate, as far as I can make out, and raising the rents of those that were left."

"Of course one is very glad he wasn't killed altogether," said a brother magistrate; "but I think it will be a lesson to other fellows of the same class not to try and make a good thing out of an Irish property. It *does not* do to bring English notions into Ireland. Irishmen won't stand them, and if you have the misfortune to hold Irish property, you must only cut your coat according to your cloth, and give up a great many ideas that might be very beneficial if carried out, but which you will carry out at the sacrifice of peace and quiet on your estate. The Irishman is a charming fellow if you humour him, but outrage his prejudices, in respect of land particularly, and he's the devil."

"Ay, and an Englishman can't do half what one of the old breed of the country can with them," said another. "They'll not stand half as much moving about from him; for they look upon everything he does through the medium of a traditional hatred quite as strong as the attachment they feel to the old races."

"It's all very well raising rents in England and telling tenants they may pay or go, their choice, where there isn't the same feeling of attachment to the land. The English have no sentiment about any of their occupations; it's all 'will it pay' with them, and if it doesn't pay they have plenty of other ways of getting a living, which we haven't over here; so that eviction and starvation, or the poorhouse, go together generally in this country. Englishmen don't understand us at all: they're much too consistent and methodical and practical and evenly balanced. The contradictions, and the inconsistencies, and the sentiments, and the unpractical poetry and unreasonableness of the Irishman make them stare; they can't understand it at all, it's so different to their own monotonous solidity and regularity and logical method."

"Gad, there's no doubt about their being unreasonable enough to make any one stare," said Sir John. "You may call it poetry if you like, but I call it damned annoying. Why, a fellow came to me yesterday who had bothered my life out for a lease till I gave him one, to tell me that his house was in a bad way, and he hoped I'd build him a new one; after getting his lease only the week before. They think they're to get whatever they ask for, and that wanting it's reason enough; and if they don't, oh! you're a tyrant, oppressor, and all the rest of it. It's not very easy for any one to understand them. They're just like a fox, or a woman, you never know which way they'll turn next."

"Oh, they're unreasonable enough, no doubt; but it's not that they don't see the force of your reasoning, though they won't take the answer you give them; they're shrewd enough to know reason when they hear it; but, like the most of us, only that they exaggerate the failing, they like to gratify their wishes at the expense of it, and not look at it if it gets in the way of a prejudice: and if you choose to ride the high horse full tilt against these prejudices and sentiments, you'll be riding to your death to a certainty."

"It was a curious thing the money being left untouched on the table. That's a thing you wouldn't have seen in England. There'd very soon have been a scramble for it when there was no one to look after it."

"There's been nothing heard of the man, I suppose, since?"

"Not a word, I believe; nor won't: the police, as usual, are 'making active exertions;' and your brother, I suppose, Hillier, is doing all he knows?"

"Oh, 'the captain,' indeed!" said Sir John, with a very dry and unbrotherly contempt; and they proceeded on their several ways.

Of course, the active exertions of the police had no more than their usual success. Another attempted murder gave fair promise of being added to that list of undetected crimes which is such a bitter satire upon English government in Ireland; and when Lord Shirley got up in his place in the House of Commons (from which Brady had been ousted on his petition), to inquire what steps were being taken to bring the would-be murderer to justice, and to show that the Government acknowledged the claim to protection of life and property in Ireland as well as in other parts of the United Kingdom, he received the usual stereotyped answer from a glib Minister, —that the authorities were using their utmost endeavours to ensure the vindication of the law; that an extra force of police had been quartered in the district, just as one might double-lock a stable-door when the horse was gone; and that various other equally puerile and senseless steps had been taken, and that the ends of justice would be defeated, if he were to indicate more precisely the nature of the means which they had thought it right to adopt. As if the ends of justice had been so completely secured in former cases, where a similar plea for reticence had been advanced, to warrant the reiteration of it on the present occasion ! And then he wound up in a neat peroration, with a high eulogium on the character and activity of the police (who are utterly unsuited, in every way, for the detection of such crimes), and expressed his fervent desire, of course, for the peace, prosperity, and happiness of the country—which desire, without efficient detective measures, was worth just about as much as such trite and fluent aspirations usually are.

Mr. Marjoribanks, meanwhile, was slowly and painfully recovering from his wound; and Larry Mc Gowan being made the hero, probably, of Ribbon meetings, or the welcome guest of sympathizing and admiring friends, under the very noses of the extra force of police who had been despatched from headquarters to lounge about the neighbourhood, to the irritation of the householders who had to pay for their support, and the secret ridicule of the murderer's accomplices. It was a sorry farce this exhibition of Government energy, sending down a couple of hundred soldiers—the Irish police are virtually soldiers—where one detective, who might have been found, perhaps, among the small shopkeepers of the district, would have been of fifty times more use. But that is the way things are done in Ireland, and then people are surprised that murder continues to be carried on with impunity.

The landlord's retirement from activity produced a lull in the excitement on the estate, and they began to wonder what the next move would be. Temporarily they had won. It remained to be seen whether he would accept defeat. Things remained for the present *in statu quo*—and it was a very demoralized *quo*. Murmuring was only suspended. There were plenty more evictions impending, and plenty of distress, with no one to relieve it. Under the Rochforts, the property used to be the envy of surrounding tenants; who, many of them, held under absentees, and had no one to apply to in want and sickness and difficulty, and who now congratulated themselves that, at least, they had a liberal absentee for head landlord, and an agent who understood them, and wouldn't turn a poor man out upon the road as long as he behaved himself. Times had sadly changed since Alan Rochfort's death, and Nora had many a petition and letter sent after her to England, detailing the want, and the misery, and the grievances which had come upon her old people. She had forgiven nearly the whole of their arrears, and sent them money and blankets and sympathy; making Bartley Mc Loughlin her almoner, and often writing to Kathleen and others of her former favourites, for intelligence of the old place.

And now a rumour springs up and spreads through the neighbourhood that Miss Nora, God bless her, was going to be married; and every one is asking, "Did she get a good match? Is he an estated gentleman? Ah! there's nothing like an estated man; he bates all the soldiers that ever were in this world." The news had been brought from Kilmorris one fair day, and it was soon confirmed on better authority than mere hearsay. Lord Shirley, Lord Mountstewart, as he very soon would be, was going to marry Miss Rochfort, and the country, high and low, were talking about it.

Lady Eleanor's mind was set at rest; and in the prospect of seeing the last of the Geraldscourt race marrying position, pedigree, and Conservative principles, like Shirley's, she could go down into her grave content.

More than two years had now elapsed since they had bade good-bye to Geraldscourt; and while Nora still retained her mourning, Shirley had not reminded her of the promise she had made him in that soft moonlight night on the terrace. Of course he had reminded her now, or he wouldn't be going to marry her; and Nora was looking forward to a return to the neighbourhood of her former home with mixed feelings of joy and sadness difficult to separate.

The tenantry on both estates were in the highest state of interest and excitement at the news, and some of the more prominent of Shirley's tenants about Mount-Stewart had set on foot a subscription for a presentation, to testify their appreciation of the way in which he discharged the duties of proprietorship towards them; other outlying estates belonging to the house joined with them; the Geraldscourt tenants begged to be allowed to contribute also; and a handsome sum was soon raised, and turned into plate and jewellery, to await their arrival at Mount-Stewart.

It is too far to go to the marriage in London—St. James's, Piccadilly. A bishop—a lovely bride, rustling with old family lace and orange flowers—a nervous Shirley—many pretty creatures in forget-me-nots and tulle—hosts of carriages in gay attire—gorgeous millinery *en fête*—then that most stupid of all the stupid entertainments which Messrs. Gunter provide, a wedding breakfast—and waiting afterwards till the greys drove off, amid shouts and slippers, to seclusion in a borrowed country-house—and then prosaic every-day life again.

It was a month or more before Shirley brought his bride to Mount-Stewart; but when he did come, preparations extraordinary had been made to give her a fitting welcome. The heir to the Mount-Stewart estates was not married every day—fortunately, perhaps, for him—and the occasion was a worthy one for all display. Kilmorris was to be illuminated: there were tallow candles stuck in lumps of putty, or cold stirabout, or other receptacles, in every window. In the town-hall festive arrangements had been made for doing justice to the fat oxen which had been sent from Mount-Stewart to celebrate the occasion; and glorious fights were confidently expected in the evening. Flags of every hue had been improvised, and suspended at every available point. Triumphal arches, with "*Cead mille failthe*"—a hundred thousand welcomes—ran up against the eye at every turn, and the whole town was assembling towards the railway station in their Sunday best, to cheer the arrival of the train.

Kilmorris was a long way from Mount-Stewart, and Newtown Mount-Stewart was their proper station; but the mayor and corporation of Kilmorris had very naturally considered that an opportunity, such as this, for impressing the townspeople with their dignity was not be thrown away, and it had been unanimously agreed, therefore, that an address from the town of Kilmorris was an indispensable part of the day's programme. Notification of their decision having been forwarded to his lordship, together with an intimation of the extreme gratification which their ancient borough would feel if they would consent to drive through the town to Mount-Stewart, they had good-naturedly consented to do so, and were now on their way from Dublin, with two or three of Shirley's friends, who were concocting a speech for him *en route*.

Nora had determined to banish all sad reminiscences from her mind for this day, at least; and the excitement of anticipated excitement helped the resolution, and imparted a brilliant bloom to her beauty, which promised a rapturous reception from the Irish crowd awaiting them.

Shirley's friends had not got much beyond the fulness of heart which prevented him expressing himself as he felt on the auspicious occasion, and as the station drew near were amusing themselves the more in playing comforters to his Job in prospect of the enthusiasm of which they were about to be the focus, when, as the train and its decorated engine came in sight of the platform, the whole party were suddenly startled by a dropping fire of small arms, which at once suggested Fenians, and turned out to be a salvo of welcoming fog-signals upon the rails. The train then glided slowly past a motley crowd upon the platform, who peered eagerly into every carriage as it passed; and the arriving party were skilfully drawn up at the red cloth point, where the mayor and corporation had taken their important stand.

Shirley and his bride step out upon the platform; the assembled multitude cheer,—(Irishmen don't know how to cheer); the Mayor in his noble suit of red, mace in hand, presses to the front, and immediately commences to read his embossed address, despite the pressure of the crowd, who jostled the reading and the read-to party on every side. Shirley takes off his hat, and listens with becoming interest, while Nora excites scarcely subdued expressions of admiration on all sides; the band of the militia strikes up its one tune, and plays it backwards and forwards unintermittently under the direction of a warm and crowded bandmaster, who has a cornopean to his own share, and is determined that, as far as his instrument and energy go, the proceedings shall not want life and spirit; and then the address comes to an end. Lady Shirley smiles her thanks, and her husband replies in a few happily chosen phrases, (I believe that is the correct term); they both shake hands with the members of the Corporation with an affability and grace which said members will unctuously dilate upon to their wives upon their return; and then there is a cry of "tenants," and some irresponsible and officious hanger-on of the programme makes the crowd open out upon a line of comfortable farmers, with each a white paper rose in his button-hole. These have to be shaken hands with also; and after that there seems nothing further to be done on the platform, and a passage is cleared to the carriage.

Such crushing and squeezing and shouting and alms-begging, forming quite a little excitement for the other passengers in the train; and then at last, amid a shower of coin from his lordship, the carriage drives off, leaving the women behind in full comment. "Ah! now, isn't she a lovely crathur? and the dress of her! did ever ye see the like? she's a rale beauty then," &c., &c. The band hurries out to despatch one last inspiriting note after the departing wheels, before receiving at their leisure the admiring applause of the populace. The tenantry, mounted on their galloping cobs, ride on before with outriders and white streamers, ragged men and ragged women hooraying, little boys scampering alongside, with an eye to business, flags fluttering, handkerchiefs waving, windows crowded, postilion bobbing and cracking his whip; and in the midst of all the clatter and enthusiasm, Nora flushed with excitement, bowing with happy smiles past the very spot where, not much more than two years before, her father had been shot, in upholding the cause of the husband by her side. It might have seemed like a triumphal procession over his grave, if she had had time to think; but fortunately she had not. A few minutes after and the town had been left behind, and they were resting from it all, and discussing the comic incidents of the platform as they hurried along through the green hedge-rows behind their mounted escort; some of whom had found already that it was the pace that killed, and been obliged to drop behind into a more leisurely trot in the rear.

It was a different kind of country altogether on this side of Kilmorris to what it was about Geraldscourt, just as Mount-Stewart itself was quite a different kind of place, and, to some tastes, not half so interesting or attractive an one as Geraldscourt. The road ran along through fine grass lands and well-bred cattle, and past well-to-do farm-houses, which Shirley or his father had either built or provided the slates and timber for. The cottages were clean, well-thatched, had gardens, some of them, and cabins were rare. The farms were large, and dwellings more scattered; and here and there evidences of good farming might be seen. The land was well-drained, and the grass of the richest and greenest; and there was quite an English or Scotch air of prosperity and comfort all along the road until you arrived at the commencement of the park wall, which enclosed the only woods to be seen in the neighbourhood, and ran alongside the road for a long way before you reached the gateway. Here more crowds were waiting, more arches, more banners, more cheering and excitement, which was prolonged all the way through the park, and culminated in a perfect furore when the carriage dashed up to the door (it is the proper thing, I believe, for a carriage to "dash" up on an occasion of the kind), when the escort wheeled round, hot and sore, and waved their hats and cheered again; when all the servants fluttered from the upper windows, the flags upon the tents joining in, and the multitudinous gathering of men and women seethed towards the entrance, where old Lord Mount-stewart was posted in his chair, and where that charming, benevolent looking old lady, Shirley's mother, was descending the steps to welcome her daughter-in-law to her future home. It was really a stirring sight; and Nora was quite overcome as she returned the old lady's warm embrace.

Mount-Stewart, mind you, was a place of no mean pretension. Even in poor, backward, barbarous, benighted Ireland, there are houses which it does not happen to everybody to become mistress of; and Mount-Stewart was of the number. Architecturally fine, geographically extensive, unlimited deer looking on in astonishment at the unwonted gathering of men and women, and tents, and horses, and other signs of excitement which no deer could understand; park slightly undulated, stretching away beyond the lake into vistas of deep woods, and under stately oaks, fern-carpeted and sheep-bestrewn; lawns, gardens, and every other mark of an external civilization, which was not belied by the interior. Servants, with their stockings not in creases—but let me see, do servants wear their stockings in the day-time? writing this in solitary rustic state, I have no leg of reference at hand, but I think they do sometimes: servants, we said, with their stockings not in creases (and in slipshod Ireland this is rare, perhaps), the powder on their hair, and not upon their coats, and eke their shoes upon their feet; in fact, not to particularize too minutely, they did possess that air of set-up smartness which fastidious English people, fresh from the great houses of their own superior country, assert that they do not find in Ireland. Then the staircase was not a mean staircase at all; nor were the proportions, or the decorations of the rooms; and the groom of the chambers was a most perfect gentlemen, and did the honours of the place in a most faultlessly agreeable manner. But Lady Mountstewart herself was the chief attraction of the whole. I should like to stop and describe her, but as she has nothing to do with our purpose I won't. She was one of those charming, gentle old ladies who have accepted age; full of mellow sweetness and refinement, breathing of sympathy, and love, and unselfishness; caring little for the world, and wrapped up, as it were, in the desire to say something kind, or do something kind to every creature who was thrown in her way; idolized by her sons, and now more than ever Nora's beau ideal of a mother.

There was very little time, however, for talking. A great deal of work had to be got through that afternoon; and the performances commenced soon after with the introduction of a deputation of tenants, to present an address of welcome and congratulation—in which they expressed the most cordial attachment to their landlord, and enumerated *seriatim* the many excellent points of his character as proprietor; his fairness, his liberality in making improvements for the benefit of the estate; the confidence and feeling of security which all alike felt under his management of the property; the facilities which he gave to any tenant who wished to dispose of his farm; his accessibilty to all complaints, preferred either to himself or to Mr. Townsend (to whose merits, as an agent, a warm tribute was also paid); his respect for their rights; the equitable compensation which was allowed for unexhausted improvements made by the tenant; and, above all, eulogising the uniform interest which all the members of his family, as well as himself, had always shown in the welfare of the tenantry by spending so much of their time among them, and returning to the estate so much of the money which they drew from it. Lady Shirley, they said, was no stranger to them; her beauty and her virtues had been well known throughout the county before affliction came upon her house; and if they had not, the love which she was capable of inspiring was amply proved by the eagerness with which her old people had come forward to contribute towards the gift which they were now jointly offering for their acceptance, &c., &c., &c.

Shirley, of course, thanked them from the bottom of his heart for the good wishes they had expressed for their happiness, the magnificent present which they had made them, and the kind expressions they had used towards himself; and he went on to say that he had always endeavoured to fulfil the duties incumbent upon proprietorship to the best of his ability, and that it was gratifying to find that his efforts appeared to have been to some extent successful.

There were some men in Ireland, he said, who, if they had their way, would banish landlords from the country altogether: mischievous agitators, who looked no further than their own love of ignorant applause, and whatever profit might be made out of it; who would hand over the country to a state of anarchy, in which no man could call his life or his property his own. But he thought he might safely say that such views found no advocates among the sensible men whom he was addressing. The great evil of the country was, that so many landlords lived out of it, and spent in England and elsewhere the money which their tenants had a right to see returned to them in the shape of material improvements, or employment of one kind or another. For his part he could not see the sense of holding property at a distance in that way. It was a bad investment for money, and without residence, and the duties and pleasures consequent upon residence, there could be no enjoyment. He would much rather sell at once. As it was, he found an infinite enjoyment in living in the midst of them, as his poor father had always done; and meetings of this kind, where the tenantry came forward spontaneously to express their goodwill and attachment, were the greatest encouragement possible to a landlord to persevere in his duty. Their country, he was sorry to say, had become notorious of late for shameful outrages in connection with property; but he was glad to know that he was addressing men who would scorn to resort to such cowardly measures for vindicating what they conceived to be their rights: fair consideration, as they knew, was always given by Mr. Townsend to every alleged grievance; and he believed he might say that no one ever went away justly dissatisfied with the redress he obtained. For himself, he could say that it should always be his endeavour to maintain the same good feeling which now existed between them, and which for long centuries had existed; and he need hardly tell them, that he was sure their interests would be as dear to Lady Shirley as they knew her former people's to have been.

A general invitation had been conveyed to the Geraldscourt tenantry to be present at the festivities at Mount-Stewart, but none of them came. They knew they were under a cloud, and stayed at home. Terence Mc Gowan, in any case, would not have shown his face, for very shame. But Kathleen Nora had expressly written to, and she had gone, accordingly, with her father and mother from Glen Annagh. Her name was not known to many of the low country people; and only for her mountain beauty, her connection with Larry Mc Gowan would have been unknown. As it was, it only created an accidental and passing interest, quite second to that produced by her personal appearance; and married women being generally known by their maiden names, Kathleen O'Hara suggested nothing beyond a very handsome young woman.

Mrs. O'Hara was very anxious for Shirley to come out. She was quite sure he must remember her after the visit he had paid them two or three years ago, and took up her husband quite shortly when he ventured to suggest a less confident reliance upon his lordship's memory for every poor tenant's face. At all events, they had Kathleen with them, and she would ensure them getting a word. Mrs. O'Hara took care that her friends and acquaintances whom she met should know the intimate terms upon which Kathleen and Lady Shirley had been in former years, and how she had made a point of her being present to-day; in fact, only that they didn't like to be too forward, they might be inside the house itself at that moment.

The presentation business was over at last, and the deputation was trickling out, after expending much wondering admiration on the interior of the hall, and enjoying some friendly conversation with their landlord and his wife; about whose winning manners they could hardly express themselves sufficiently to the eager groups who were asking questions all round.

Then Shirley appeared at the entrance again, coming out among them to introduce Lady Shirley to their nearer gratification, followed by others of the party in the house, whose gala costumes struck a perfect awe into the simple peasant mind : the ladies', of course; I don't think that Shirley's brothers had any element of awe about them. Younger brothers are generally a failure; perhaps not younger brothers particularly, but brothers generally. You take a fancy to some very nice, gentlemanlike, good-looking, sensible fellow, conceive almost a friendship for him perhaps, and in course of time come across the rest of his family; and find a Burlington Arcade soldier, perhaps, for one brother, a Grub Street author, very likely, for another, or a city clerk smelling of sugar and dressed *à la* Stock Exchange, or some other profession-stamped monster, perfectly different to your friend. Shirley's brothers suffered more from negative faults; but then negative qualities do make positively uninteresting young men, who are quite as tiresome and irritating as more objectionably defined characters. Individually, I should much prefer to live with a common fiend than with a well-meaning, good-hearted, amiable, and insipid idiot. These remarks, however, are not very much to our present purpose, which is to mingle freely, as the newspapers have it, with the rotating crowds in the gardens and upon the lawn.

Affability was the order of the day; and Mrs. O'Hara lost no time in intercepting a share for herself and her party. Nora's face grew even a degree brighter yet, when her eyes fell upon Kathleen's retiring advance, and she held out her hand with all her old unaffected cordiality in a way which perfectly charmed the casual lookers-on around. I say casual advisedly, for in Ireland we don't mob and stare at the victims of these exceptional occasions in the way which, from blushing experience, we have found to be habitual in more civilized lands. Our natural barbarity of manners has not been sufficiently stamped out by contact as yet, and, therefore, on such occasions we assume a respectful courtesy of distance, and avoid any approach to what, in our simplicity, we should consider intrusive rudeness.

Nora had all sorts of questions to ask about

Geraldscourt, and sympathy to express for Terence, and other matters to talk about to Kathleen; far more than she had time for at present, in consideration of that free mingling which she thought would be expected from her; and, therefore, after telling her that she must see her again before they went away, she swept on to other groups, leaving Kathleen blushing at having attracted so much notice before so many people, and Mrs. O'Hara looking round to see if it had been duly observed; while old Thady followed her admiringly with his eyes, instituting invidious comparisons between her and his own daughter, who, with like advantages of dress, would have run her very close, he thought.

The progress having been completed, there was an adjournment to the house again for tea, while the old women crowded into the tea and bread-and-butter tents, and the men determined towards the spacious marquee where dinner was to come off.

That important event commenced soon after: Shirley at one end of the table—his agent at the other. There were healths and speeches by wealthy farmers, who praised the landlord, and praised the agent, and praised themselves. The landlord responded, flattered the tenants, complimented the agent, and excused himself. And then the agent rose and congratulated the tenants, congratulated himself, and congratulated the country on having such a landlord. It was charming to see such perfect harmony of sentiments on a point which is believed to be a source of discord in Ireland.

Shirley then left them to themselves, and found that Nora had been occupying her time before dinner in interviewing Kathleen, as to the disturbances which had lately arisen about Geraldscourt.

It was a great change entirely, Kathleen said. The people were very wishful for her back, and though they had tided over their troubles for the time, she was afraid they had not seen the end of them. Terence had not been like himself, she said, at all since that bad work of Larry's, and so bitter he was against the party doings that brought him to it, she was afeard of her life he'd come to harm himself some day.

Nora suggested that they had better leave the estate altogether, and take a farm near Mount-Stewart somewhere: her husband would easily find one for them. But Kathleen thought of the new house, just finished, by the birch copse and the rocky stream, which Terence was so attached to, and knew that he would rather stay upon that spot, where his childhood had been spent, and put up with the hardest terms, than exchange its poor mossy soil for any lowland loam. Nora accordingly said no more.

It was time then to dress for dinner; and dinner over, there was a visit to the dancing-tent, where a fiddler, mounted up aloft, was dispensing his jokes and his jigs to an interminably bobbing, laughing audience; who ceased their steps for more cheering when the house party entered, and then at it again with a real Irish enjoyment, to show how they *could* dance, for the admiration of the quality: and then that long fatiguing day came to an end, and the shouting, and the laughter, and the merriment, died away before the rising sun and the wakening of the early birds amidst the glitter of the dawn.

CHAPTER X.

When Kathleen returned again to her home, she found a surprise awaiting her. The old house was deserted. Terence was dandling her cherub at the door of the new one above, and the old woman smoking her pipe over the new hearth. The stream was sparkling along in all the brightness of a joyful morning sun, the grass among the rocks was never greener, the air never clearer, the view never more beautiful; and her face was radiant with beaming joy and freshness, as Terence threw his arm round her, and welcomed her home—to their new home. The baby had then to be hung over and kissed, and hung over and gazed upon, and kissed again; and then she had leisure to recount, in the graphic way which comes natural to Irish peasants, the gay doings at which she had lately been present; Miss Nora's kindness, inquiries, and offers.

"But I knew, Terence dear, you'd not leave the old place, while there was any livin' in it at all."

"It's true for ye, Kathleen asthore," answered Terence. "It 'd take a big offer entirely that 'd bring me away out o' this, where the family's been this hundred years an' more. It's a poor soil, but I'd not be content to change it for many a better; and so with the best o' thanks to Miss Nora for her kindness, we'll just stay where we are, Kathleen, till we're put out of it, and no thanks to us. With the new house raised over us now, with the help o' God, we'll have great happiness yet,"

With that he kissed her once more; and if the future could have been augured from the present, there would have been a deal of joy and happiness in store for them.

"But you didn't hear what they're sayin' since you were away," Terence went on. "The new landlord's goin' to quit they're talkin', whenever he'll be got round to that; and it's what we'll have an agent then, I suppose. It's bad changin' so often. A man 'll never know what'll be the next move, and can't be secure with himself that way, when he'll not have a lease to stand by."

"Oh, Terence, don't let's think about that to-day," said Kathleen, imploringly. "If trouble's to come, it'll come soon enough, without our thinkin' on it; and maybe when his honour there leaves the country we shall have peace again, please God."

Terence was angry with himself for having stirred up a thought to mar her present happiness, and did his best then to soothe it away; and they went out into the bright sunshine, and wandered over their little farm together, and made projects for the future, and wasted a great deal more time than Terence was usually guilty of throwing to loss; and then he went off about his work, and Kathleen returned to help her mother-in-law to put down the dinner, and to make a proper disposition of their household gods.

The report that Mr. Marjoribanks was going to

leave the country was true. Directly he was fit to be moved, change of scene was prescribed. His energy was broken, and he had no longer any desire to live in a country where he could be fired at in the very presence of the police, and the man who fired the shot escape with impunity. In England there was, at all events, some fear of detection to keep would-be criminals in check—in Ireland apparently there was none. The people laughed at authority which was never enforced, and it was evidently hopeless to do anything among a set of people to whom law was unknown. His attempt had been a failure; but as a speculation he still had hopes of making the property a success. He should not endanger his own life any more among such a set of lawless savages, but they should not on that account be allowed to continue on as before. And in pursuance of such resolution, as soon as he was able to hold a pen, he wrote to Dublin for an agent—the one whom he had found there having declined the post.

It was not easy to find a man willing to undertake the agency under the peculiar circumstances of the property; but at last young Mr. Puller, of the land-agency firm of Puller, Devile, Puller, and Baker, declared that fear was a thing unknown to his manly bosom, and that he himself would offer for the place.

Mr. Puller, junior, was young in age, but old in shrewdness, not troubled with moral scruples to any great extent, anxious for independence, and experienced in the disinclination to return usually shown by Englishmen who had mismanaged Irish properties to within an ace of their lives; moreover the place promised a pleasant residence, sport, absolute freedom of action, and he would ensure its being a remunerative post. He therefore proposed himself, was gladly accepted, and went down forthwith to spy out the land.

Mr. Marjoribanks had already left, and all his instructions were therefore given by letter, and carried out or not as the judgment of his agent recommended. The head landlord, writing from England, had no idea of showing any leniency to tenants who had acted towards him as they had; and I believe I am correct in saying that Mr.

Marjoribanks was the very man who wrote to his agent desiring him to inform the tenants that their threats of shooting him (the agent) would not, in the slightest degree, intimidate their landlord.

The new agent, however, began by feeling his way, with some experience of the ground upon which he was treading; and the tenants, satisfied, apparently, with their late victory, were more docile than he expected. They had asserted themselves, and now they were inclined to be good boys. Of course, there was an infinite variety of reasons alleged why they should not pay up the arrears due, and why time should be allowed them to collect the bit of rent which they had in their pockets at the moment; but though Mr. Puller was a young man recently from town, they did not get over him in that way, and they very soon, therefore, ceased to make the attempt. As to the arrears, he was not so eager about them; for his salary being so much per cent. (five per cent.) on the yearly income, the collection of arrears was not material to his interests. In many cases, therefore he represented the advisability of foregoing them, in consideration of punctual payment for the future. Evictions he stopped; they were dangerous, and would not add to the rental immediately. Leases he encouraged; there was a bonus accompanying them, if desired. Expiring leases were renewed on the same terms. The harsh measures he deplored as the landlord's; the lenient ones he naturally extolled as his own. On the whole, his somewhat corrupt management seemed at first to promise tranquillity, and Mr. Brady's practice began to fall off. Mr. Puller was often reproached for this by his friend (for Mr. Brady was a friend of long standing—they had been boys at school together); and Mr. Puller would say that he had had his turn—that he must not complain. Funny Mr. Puller!

So things went on for some months. Terence applied for a lease, and the application was coldly received. He was a brother of the Mc Gowan whom the police had failed to lay their hands upon, and, as such, it might not be desirable to trust him with a lease.

A few months afterwards he applied again, but

this time, for some reason or other, the request was received with contemptuous astonishment.

"You are about the last man on the estate I should think of giving a lease to," said the agent.

"And why so, sir?" asked Terence. "Your honour" was too good for such as this man, who, he heard, made poor tenants pay him money for getting anything they wanted from him. Bartley McLoughlin even had given up the post of bailiff in disgust.

"Why?" repeated the agent. "Do you suppose I haven't heard the sort of man you are? Do you think I'm going to secure any man in possession on this estate whose brother is a would-be murderer, and who wouldn't be above doing the same himself, by all accounts?"

"And is one man to be answerable for what another man does that's his brother?" asked Terence, with scarcely subdued anger.

"No; but he's answerable for what he does himself, though. You've forgotten, I suppose, that beating you gave Mr. Brady one time, when his father was standing for the county against your late landlord's candidate? Your memory is short, perhaps?"

"It's not short at all, sir. But, maybe, Mr. Brady didn't tell you what got him that same beating. Did he tell you that it was for offering to lay hands on a poor girl that had no way of defendin' herself agen him—the very same that's now my own wife, thank God!"

"Not a very likely story," said Mr. Puller, incredulously; thinking, however, at the same time, that it was not at all an improbable version of that little affair which Brady had related to him one day after Terence had passed them, with the object of putting a spoke in his wheel.

Terence felt very much inclined at that moment to repeat the operation on Mr. Brady's friend for daring to treat his word so lightly; but there was a good strong piece of furniture between them, and considerations of prudence, after a slight struggle, triumphed over the more indignant man.

"Ay, but it *is* a likely story, Mr. Puller," he exclaimed; "and what's more, it's the truth; and ne'er a man yet but yourself ever accused me to my face of tellin' a lie, and wasn't right sorry that ever the word passed his mouth! I'm a poor man, sir, but I'm an honest man, I hope, and a poor man's word 'll oftentimes be every bit as good as a gentleman's; and a deal better than some o' those that goes by the names o' gentlemen, an's no more gentlemen than rubbishy weeds is garden flowers, for all they're lyin' in the same bed with other. If Mr. Brady 'd had any call to the name, he wouldn't have been on for that work, and he wouldn't be strivin' to ruin me with my landlord now, so he wouldn't."

"I really can't pretend to enter into a discussion of Mr. Brady's claims with you," said the agent. "I only know that I see no reason for giving you a lease; and a lease you will not get, so there's an end of it."

Terence, however, was not willing that the interview should be ended so summarily, and insisted that the landlord had promised him a lease; that he had built a house and begun reclaiming work on the strength of it, and that if he was not to get it now it would be rank injustice, and that he would apply to the head landlord himself about it.

Mr. Puller smiled pleasantly at the threat. He knew that Mr. Marjoribanks was in Madeira for his health, and not likely to return alive, so that his control of the property at the present moment was absolute, and admitted of whatever treatment might conduce the most to his advantage without incurring unnecessary risk. The intimation, however, of an appeal from his authority incensed him further against Terence, who was always too honest a man in speech and appearance for him to have any great sympathy with, and he therefore, after the first sweet emotion of contemptuous security, rejoined angrily,—

"You may apply to Mr. Marjoribanks if you please, and if he chooses to sanction it, well and good. But all I can tell you now is that I am in charge of the estate at the present, and that while I am in charge you will have no lease. You have your answer. You may go. Do you hear me? Go! You're a troublesome fellow, sir, and I shall keep my eye upon you, mind that!"

Conscious how one-sided a contest he was engaged in, Terence could only deliver his feelings of one parting protest against such a way of treating a tenant who always paid his rent to the day; and turning upon his heel resentfully, he left the agent's previous dislike ripening into a sort of vindictive aversion.

A rogue must feel for an honest man much the same kind of natural repulsion which a burglar may be supposed to entertain towards a policeman's lantern. The sense of himself and his deeds become too vivid to be pleasant under such a straight-forward open light, and the fear of detection in the one, and the sense of inferiority with which the other becomes oppressed, may fairly be supposed to create similar feelings of aversion towards the respective causes of these uncomfortable sensations. At all events Mr. Puller, proved rogue or no, had no great love for Terence Mc Gowan after this interview; and, easily imagining how he would be handled by him amongst his neighbours, and how his power might be undermined by men of the sort, he would have been only too glad of an excuse to get him off the estate. But such an excuse was not easy to find. His rent was regularly paid, and his industry none could deny. He was reclaiming bog, and improving his farm in every possible way; and Mr. Puller always passed his land with a feeling of irritation. He was distantly respectful, too, and seemed to have forgotten the refusal of his lease; and it was not even possible to accuse him of Fenian sympathies: for which, on adjoining estates, there had been evictions of late.

Terence always kept aloof from rebellion: not that the instinct of nationality was less strong in him than in men like Nolan, for whose idle hands Satan found ready mischief in political incendiarism; who, after the manner of their kind, were anxious to find other shoulders to bear the blame of their condition, when they had only themselves to thank for it; and who, in many cases—in Nolan's especially—were joining loudly in a cry of Ireland for the Irish, which, if successful, would have left them out in the cold altogether—seeing that they could boast no connection at all with the original possessors of the soil: whose lineal descendants it would be no easy thing to discover at the present day. Terence was as good an Irishman as any of them, and if there had been any prospect of success, there is not a doubt but what he would have liked to see his country taking a position of her own among the nations. But in common with most of the sensible men of the district who assembled at Geraldsbridge post-office to hear inflammatory articles read out of the so-called national papers, which a wise Government permits to be sown broadcast through the country for the enlightenment of the lower classes, he felt that without the assistance of a crowned head, as they put it, they would only be running their heads against a wall, and that it was no patriotism to disturb the country without hope of any successful result.

There were very many, however, in whom the sentiments and stirring pictures of the newspapers produced a much more enthusiastic ardour, and afforded the text for indignant declamation and passionate thrills of noble and mistaken patriotism over their turf-fires in the winter evenings. There being no resident landlord there was no employment at the Big House; and what young men there were in the country were, therefore, left without occupation, and a ready prey to agitation. An American fellow had been going about the parish, and Father Hugh had warned them from the altar to have nothing to say to him, not to let him into their houses; but nevertheless he was made welcome at many a hearth, and his promises of glory and freedom and independence eagerly drank in by his ignorant audience. The estate was soon to be their own. There was to be a general distribution of all the surrounding properties. Every one would have his share. No more landlords—no more agents—no more exterminating Englishmen. The reign of oppression and tyranny would be over and Ireland's millenium arrived, if they would only join heart and soul in this new effort to free their country from the degrading chains which she had worn so long. There were thousands of their brave countrymen coming across the sea to help them, and this time they would strike to some purpose, and show what Ireland's sons could do in Ireland's cause—the cause of their beloved trodden-down country—(immense applause).

It is not to be supposed that Mr. Puller's

rule was so absolutely agreeable as to occasion no discontent upon the property. There were innumerable reasons why sedition should find a not uncongenial soil around Geraldscourt now. The head landlord, the agent grieved to say, insisted upon having his rents punctually paid, whether the season was good or bad; and moreover, in order that the agent's percentage might profit, he had insisted upon a rise in many of the rents which had not been raised at first, and therefore there was now no property at that end of the county—scarcely even attorney Brady's—so highly rented as this of Geraldscourt; which formerly had been held on such exceptionally easy terms. Then there had been harsh and arbitrary agreements forced upon some for purposes of the agent's own; unwarrantable ejectments, as he grew bolder, ventured upon for the purpose of installing other tenants who had made it worth his while to run the risk, and a general system of extortion practised, which the landlord, far away from England, had no means of knowing, and which did not tend to tranquillity upon the estate. Mr. Puller, in fact, generally drove at a gallop now, when out upon the property, particularly up the hills. Hopes, too, had been of late excited by the injudicious utterances of certain English statesmen, and there was a general belief prevalent that some great change in the land laws was impending, which even if their rebellious patriotism met with no success, would indefinitely improve their position to the detriment of the landowners; and therefore, by anticipation, they began to bear themselves in an independent and triumphant manner which very easily took offence. They laughed at the English Government; despising it for its confessed weakness, as judged by results, and ascribing coming concession solely to the fear that if they were not wise in time, more than they could offer would be wrung from them by force.

On the whole, therefore, there was a dangerous feeling abroad, which it was not wise to tamper with; which caused men to talk below their breath upon the broad high road; to meet in knots and groups, and wear defiant looks when passed by any magistrate or landlord, or other person in authority. Rents were sullenly paid in; in many instances were not paid at all, but refused point blank, and collection was, perforce, deferred. Society seemed trembling on the brink of a coming change; and it was at this singularly inopportune moment that Mr. Puller's evil genius prompted him to put a rent upon some land which Terence Mc Gowan had recently reclaimed, and from which he had, as yet, received not a shilling of return for capital expended.

He had borne a good deal in one way or another since Alan Rochfort's death, but this last straw broke down his patience; and unconsciously, perhaps, infected by the atmosphere of resistance prevailing at the time, he at once refused to pay.

"Very well," Mr. Puller said quietly and contentedly, declining to listen to remonstrances; and on the next day a notice to quit was served.

From the moment of receiving that notice, Terence became a changed man. He was like one possessed. The sympathy and indignation of his neighbours had no effect upon him; he scarcely seemed to heed them. Poor Kathleen, in her distress at the prospect before them, was quite frightened at times at the look which his face wore; at the fierce tenderness with which he pressed her to his heart, or caught her children to his knee. He would start up in bed at night, as if from some frightful dream, drops of perspiration bursting from his forehead, and then would sink down again with a muttered oath, and passively suffer the attempts she made to soothe him. The children would hush their tiny prattle now when he strode into the house, and shrink away into the corner, instead of, as heretofore, running up to him to be caressed. The old mother looked silently at him, and shook her head, as he sat savagely brooding over the hearth; and when Kathleen timidly approached, and put her arm about him, and tried to win him to himself again, she met with no response—a tremor, perhaps, through his frame, but nothing more. His whole being seemed concentrated in one enchaining thought; and from his eyes there gleamed so fierce a light at times, that she thought, poor girl, he must be going mad—and perhaps he was!

CHAPTER XI.

Days passed away, and Terence's strange mood continued, growing only more intense, and dark, and fixed. His old tenderness was gone; his energies seemed perverted into some hidden channel; he avoided company; his trembling wife, even, he would put from him, and start away into the darkness of night alone sometimes, and not come back till she had watched and watched herself to sleep in waiting for him in the dim and shadowy firelight, imagining fearful things, which thought scarce yet defined. At last he started up at dawn one morning, after a night of troubled sleep, and, merely saying that he was going to Kilmorris, left the house without touching food. Poor Kathleen watched him, weeping, from the door until he turned the corner, and then sat down before the fire, and found no comfort even in her children, who clamoured to be taken up, and lisped their infant sympathy to little purpose. A shuddering dread had come upon her lately,—a nameless, awful fear; and she could scarcely bear her husband from her sight, although she often had to bear it, and wait and listen to every passing sound with a beating, terrible suspense, which dreaded, and yet longed, to recognize his step. His errand to Kilmorris, what could it be for? Her timid question as he left the house, had not been answered; he had thrust her from him so almost fiercely, so unlike his former self, that she had burst into tears, reproachful, pitying, desolate—that his love for her should cease was worse than all; anything, almost *anything*, but that—and he had passed quickly out, without looking at her or speaking any word to her more.

It was possible—yes, it must be so—that he was going to Mount-Stewart. They had talked, or rather she had talked, about it more than once, and tried to make him take an interest in the recollection of the offer they had had from Lady Shirley on her first arrival in the county. Kathleen had said that she would write, and he had not forbidden it. She wished she had. Why did she wish it? She hardly knew. It would have saved some anxious thought, perhaps; but now, if he was going there, it would do as well. But *was* he going there? Her heart misgave her, though she tried to think he was; and as she rocked her baby to and fro, and gazed into the fire, her face was the index to a very sad and troubled soul. Was this the life she had pictured to herself with Terence in her happy girlhood, when first his manly, handsome face had won her love? Better, far better, that he had never seen her; but for her he might now be happy in the old house below, secure in the possession of the bit of land he loved so well. This trouble was all young Mr. Brady's mean revenge; she felt quite sure of that, and only for her Terence would never have had a word with him at all; but when she looked at his little namesake on the floor, who promised to be the very image of his father, she couldn't bring herself to wish they never had been married; and she sighed a heavy sigh as her eyes turned back again to the fire, and her thoughts wandered off to the days when trouble was unknown, when they had loitered by the evening loch, or by the leafy stream in the soft spring-time, when all was joy and love and happiness around, awakening sweet responsive echoes in their own two hearts. It was all over now—a beautiful and buried dream—and she shut her eyes in sheer despair at thinking what might be to come.

That was a long, long morning; and when dinner-hour did arrive at last there was no appetite to meet it. The afternoon was all as long, as hour after hour of the bleak November day dragged through its weary course, and Terence came not back. The wild wind roaring through the woods, the blasts that whirled the scattered leaves, the crested torrent boiling down the glen, the cloud-rack tossed about the dying sun, and the pale white moon contrasted in the further blue, were all the sights and sounds which Kathleen heard and saw as she braved the fury of the gale to look along the road and see him coming perhaps.

Night saddened over all at length; the firelight grew brighter to the falling darkness, and at last he came. Unconscious of the pace he had been walking to outstrip his thoughts, the hair upon his forehead lay blackly matted with perspiration streams. His face was flushed; his eyes seemed all on fire with a wild unnatural light, as if he had been drinking; and as he advanced upon them from the door, instinctively they shrank away in silent fear, and left the fire to his absent, glaring gaze alone. In a husky voice he called for water, nor noted who it was that brought it, but drank a long deep draught and threw the porringer aside, and glared into the fire as before. Poor Kathleen moved about the room in trembling silence, unable to sit still, afraid to speak, and hushing any slightest cry from the little things who clung about her and stared in large-eyed terror at their father's mood.

The old mother took them to their bed at last, and Kathleen stayed with Terence in the room, leaning up against the dresser with her hands clasped and her whole anxious interest absorbed in his dark form and half-turned features, as he sat there fiercely silent still before the glowing embers on the hearth.

At length with a sudden impulse,—whether that his features for a moment changed their dark expression, or some strange thought came over her,— she moved towards him quickly, laid her hand lightly upon his shoulder, and called him gently by his name.

"Terence, won't you speak to me?—won't you speak to your own Kathleen, that was your happy wife until now, and that's like to die for the want of the kind word that was always ready without the askin', up to this? Ah! Terence *dear*, look up now, and speak to me. It's frightened entirely I am to see you this way these days back, my brave husband that was and is; for *I*'ll never be no other than what I always was—your lovin' wife, Terence."

"Ay, and it's that very thought, Kathleen, that drives me to it," he exclaimed, in a hard, hoarse voice, without looking at her, but clenching his hands fiercely as he spoke.

"To what? Oh! Terence—to what?" cried Kathleen, sinking down on her knees beside him, clasping his hand in her own, and looking up into his face with impassioned eagerness and dread.

He was silent. His brow contracted more savagely than ever, and she hung upon his lips in vain. The shrieking of the storm without was all the answer she received.

"Terence! Terence!" she cried, in a broken, piteous voice. "What's this at all that's come over you, my husband? What fearful thought is this that you're loth to tell to me, your wife, that you never had a secret from before? It's bad; it must be bad, Terence, or I'd be let to share it with you. Ah! quit thinkin' on it, and be your own brave self again, and we'll be happy yet. Miss Nora 'll give us land, and we'll have a snug wee house, and the childer round us, and forget that ever trouble came upon us here at all. Won't you listen, Terence dear? You'd listen to me once when there was ne'er a cloud upon the love you had for me. Is it all away so soon—so soon, Terence?" and she drew still closer to him and clasped his unresisting hand, and looked into his face with a most touching, pleading earnestness. But Terence didn't look at her. He couldn't trust his firm resolve to meet that imploring face which he couldn't but be conscious of upturned to his; and he fixed his eyes away.

Kathleen sank back, her tears no longer kept in check by the tension of her feelings, and she sobbed out bitterly—

"If e'er a one had told me that it'd ever come to this between us, Terence, I'd never have believed them. An' it's what it never would only for some awful thought that's in your mind this minute, that frights yourself at nights, and scares my very life with dread to think of. As God's above us, Terence, you're on for doin' something there'll be no forgiveness for in this world or the next! Think o' that, Terence; it's an awful thing to come under the anger o' God; and never mind what they done to us, with his help we'll bear it."

"Is it 'never mind' to be robbed o' the house a man's raised with his own toil and money?" cried Terence, starting up in great excitement; "to be forced to quit the spot he was bred and born in, and his father and his father's father before him again, that he's put the labour o' years into, and that he got no recompense but a rent put on him for—to be driven out to starve upon the road for one rascal's pleasure, and he's to never mind and bear it all, and see his wife starvin' with her little childer before his face, and turn his back upon the old fields that he's loved ever since he was a cub of a boy, and not move hand nor foot to give the scoundrel that 'd do it a notion that the man he'd do it on's a man, and has the strength of a man, and 'll use it too! Listen to me, Kathleen: I've sworn to have a bloody revenge on that agent fellow below, and I'll never break my oath."

A furious wild blast burst in the loosely-fastened door that moment as he spoke, and caused Kathleen to start back with sudden fear, as she looked expecting she scarce knew what, to follow. To Terence it seemed to point the way, and he moved towards the outer darkness as if to put an end to further questioning.

In a moment Kathleen's thoughts came rushing back, and she clung about him with passionate imploring words, entreating him to stay, to think what would his poor wife and children do; but that thought seemed only to confirm him in his purpose, and lit up his haggard unshaven face and sunken eyes with a look so fiercely wild that she shrank before it as a tender flower before a blasting heat. Still she kept her hold upon his arm, heedless of the violence of the storm which was bursting through the open door, adding riot and desolation to the scene; clinging to him with the strength and agony of despair, and pouring out her heart in tears, and prayers, and broken, choking, passionate entreaties, instinct with a very ecstasy of mingled love and terror.

At last he freed himself and broke away, and as she stood wringing her hands before the open door, the wind catching up her loosened hair and blowing it madly from her face, the scudding clouds for a moment cleared across the moon, a silver gleam shone down from the pure sky above, and she could see his tall, dark figure stoop below the bank, and as he rose again and strode away across the darkening field the last faint ray just caught the barrel of a gun. With a sharp, short, fearful cry she sprang forward as if to follow him, but a faint dizzy sickness came upon her; she tottered forward a few steps only, and sank down helpless upon the causeway stones.

* * * *

Midnight was long passed, but the gleam from the cottage windows still streamed out upon the night, and the two women's figures within still watched and watched in unspeakable dread which mocked at sleep and rest, and stamped upon their thoughts in hideous characters one only word— REVENGE!

It was no time for tears. Pale, sickly Horror led the hours on, and gave to every minute such ghastly occupation that no room was left for tearful thought. The falling gale brought sudden voices ever and anon to stir up palpitating fears, and moaned itself away in dismal plaints about the gloomy woods below, death-strewn with fallen trees. And once the latch seemed lifted, and the breath was held in mute suspense; but nothing came of it. The fancied steps outside were heard no more, and terror was hushed again into its dread repose. But hark! what sound is carried past upon the courier wind? *A shot!* There could be no mistake. They both had heard it, and it rang a death-knell in their hearts—the knell of joy in life for evermore!

The agony of those succeeding moments! the speechless horror which each confronted in the other's face, and which sent their eyes and thoughts to heaven in despairing prayer! the drooping misery of silent anguish which contrasted in Kathleen with the other's wailing, louder woe! and then that more intense and fearfully prolonged suspense which followed!

It had been a night of deep and terrible emotions, and now its culminating horror was at hand. A heavy step is hurrying up the stony path. Kathleen starts from her stupor, with a faint gleam of hope struggling through the deadly pallor of her face; but she has scarcely risen from her seat when the door is broken violently in through lock and latch, and a ruffian, whom she hardly recognizes as her husband, staggers into the room, and stares from one to the other in a half-stupefied, bewildered manner. With an eager terrified look she springs towards him, but with a sudden shriek stops short. A chilly horror runs through all her frame—the firelight flickers upon fresh spattered *blood;* and wildly pointing to it, she falls down senseless at his feet.

CHAPTER XII.

THE horrors of that night-watch, and the anxiety of days which had preceded them, were too much for the endurance of Kathleen's brain. For days and days she raved deliriously in high fever, at one time hanging upon her husband's neck, as she thought, with tender, endearing tones, such as once were all their language to each other; at another, shrinking in abject terror from that same husband, glaring upon her through the darkness as a red-handed blood-stained murderer. Who shall depict the fantastic horror of those fevered visions which a loosed imagination conjured up from that dread past? or why should they be depicted? We have surely had enough of horrors.

From Mount-Stewart, Nora had heard, of course, and read with deep concern, the tragic end of Kathleen's happiness; had written her a letter full of sympathy and kindness, and, receiving no answer, had sent a special messenger to find her out. A nurse was provided by her orders, and doctors—anything she wanted they were to let her have, and frequently send word what progress she was making. It was hard to make progress, however, through such distempered dreams as hers; and the waking would be no gliding of the storm-tossed ship into a sudden calm.

Terence was still at large, hunted and pursued from point to point like a doubling hare: wandering by the shores of lonely lochs; making his couch upon the heather, or in recesses of the woods, or in caves among the mountains far away; revisiting by stealth the neighbourhood of his home to glean tidings of Kathleen's state, which he had heard of from one or another of the scouts who kept him supplied with food at certain spots; and torn with a longing agony of grief, which found fit company in the fiery hell of thought into which remorse and conscious shame and degradation had turned his brain. His was no nature to glory in a deed of violence, and court his fellows' applause for the blood upon his hands, which had dyed away for ever his lost self-respect. His passion had gone out in the green and ghastly flame its own violence had lighted; and he shunned all contact with any who had known him as he was before that demon grasp laid hold upon his very being, and constrained him from himself to do a deed it mocked him for as soon as done. He had fallen but too consciously from that high level from which a few short days before he could look with scorn and hatred upon the deeds and thoughts of men like Nolan and his fellow-ruffians. He was of their number now—had distanced some of them, perhaps, in ungoverned cruelty and blood: he, who had preached to others, and affected to deplore his brother's guilt as bringing shame and sorrow upon all his kin—he was now meanly skulking from the law an outcast from the company of honest men, a branded murderer, a degraded wretch, who could never face the day again! The thought was maddening.

Where now was that upright consciousness of persevering industry which once had made him hold his head so high, and denounce the listless, idle life around him? The very idlest sluggard of them all could point a finger at him now, and turn the murderer from his door. The very house and land that caused it all, he could find it in his heart to loathe. Had it been ten thousand times as dear he would have freely lost it now to feel once more the elastic sense of energy and life which ever since that night had been a stranger to his thoughts. Waking or sleeping, lying down or rising up, that fell shadow would pursue and darken every thought, until, as he stood sometimes upon the edge of frowning steeps, or looked into the deep, dark waters of the mountain tarns, a something whispered,—

"Why not end it all? Is life at such a price worth having? See, the waters only wait to close upon your misery, and quench for ever all these maddening thoughts and hideous phantoms which henceforth will wait upon your going out and coming in, and follow you, no matter should you cross the seas and save the hangman's shame, and din remembrance through your brain with never-ceasing gloomy pertinacity!"

He listened, and he acquiesced, and, coward-wise, he still held back. Was it not a coward's part, perhaps, to shrink from lying on the bed himself had made? Would another crime shut out from hell the former? Was he not still a man, though loaded with a damning sense of guilt? Might life not yet be made to expiate the recollection of this accursed stain which seas would not wash out? Could happiness be possible again? Would Kathleen ever look upon him, except to loathe and hate his very sight?

"Ah! Kathleen, Kathleen, my poor, poor wife," he cried out in his agony, "why didn't I heed your darlin' voice when you bid me not go from you that time? It isn't this way I'd be now, skulkin' like some vermin animal in holes and caves, if I'd mind my own angel wife; it isn't far away like this I'd be, and you lyin' on your bed, that, maybe, you'll ne'er rise again from, that your own husband brought you to with his murderin', bloody work. God forgive me for it, Kathleen dear! Will you ever speak to me again, mavourneen, if you're spared, by the help o' God, to the childer? Ay, the childer!" he repeated; and his head drooped. "The poor wee things!

What 'll they be thinkin' o' their father when they 'll be grown up, and people 'll be castin' it up to them what he done? I'll never see them no more. Ah! but I'd like to get one sight of her with the two about her before I'd go; but it'll never be!" and the prospect of utter severance from all that quiet former happiness which came so vividly upon him now, contrasting with the darkness and desolation and shame of the future, temporarily overcame all other thoughts; he covered his face with his hands, and the lone rocks, from their misty veil, looked down upon the shedding of a strong man's bitter tears.

The active exertions of the police failed, of course, to trace him to a capture, and it was believed at last that he must have escaped out of the country. The looks exchanged between the country people when his name was mentioned, implied a better knowledge of his movements; but no information was supplied to counteract the impression prevailing among the members of the force. The sympathy of the neighbourhood was entirely with him, and wherever he might have presented himself for shelter or concealment it would have been afforded. The only man who really regretted the agent's fate was young Brady, with whom he had been dining on the evening of his murder. But Mr. Brady's power to detect was, unfortunately, not equal to his desire for detection; and for three or four weeks no clue beyond vague rumours had been found.

At last one morning it was conveyed anonymously to the astonished sergeant of police at Geraldsbridge Barracks that Terence Mc Gowan was at that moment in the vicinity of Glen Annagh; that he had passed the night in the Pol-a-vady Caves, below the Hanging Rock: and that, in all probability, he would remain there in concealment during the day.

Here was a most unlooked-for opportunity for making sure of the large reward advertised by Government for his capture; and the sergeant, worthy man, called the head-constable, and showed him the letter, and they congratulated each other over their prospects. Intelligence of the fact was conveyed with all speed and secrecy to Captain Hillier, and so flustered was he by the unexpected nature of the announcement that he forgot his personal safety so far as to say that he would accompany them; doubtless with the intention of giving them the benefit of his strategic recollections as a captain in Her Majesty's Line. On second thoughts, however, he bade them God speed, and remained at home.

As the capture was not likely to be made without considerable risk of their lives, Terence Mc Gowan being a powerful man, and it might well be supposed a desperate man now, the whole police force of six turned out, and, fully armed and loaded, marched through the village to the lively measure of their own excited anticipations,—those of them who knew on what errand they were bent; it had not been confided to all, for fear that even the mysterious heart of a vigilant policeman might not be proof against a feeling of elation likely to betray their interests by some physiognomical incontinence. Of course they headed, with business-like indifference, in the opposite direction to that in which the quarry lay; and the inhabitants having been accustomed of late to an ostentatious activity in patrolling on the part of the guardians of the public peace, thought that they were merely making the periodical display of their figures which the duties of their station required, gave them therefore the desired meed of admiration and passed on. This imposing martial array, however, was very soon broken up, and the sergeant's eager excitement carried off his legs into a double across the mountains on the very first opportunity. It was not every day that he had the chance of laying hands upon a real live prey of this kind, and the possible prospect of one day seeing his picture in the public prints as the Irish policeman who captured the murderer, no doubt contributed in a great measure to the podocean zeal with which hill after hill was surmounted in his avenging hurry, his fellow-Eumenides panting at his heels.

Some circumspection was necessary in approaching the spot, for there were means of egress at more than one point of the rocky gorge on which the caves opened. Most of them had been formed by the action of the stream, which, as the name implied, disappeared from view underground for some distance here, fretting along through arches hung with stalactites glittering in the chance rays of light breaking in from overhead, and wadable by stooping and crawling in some places, all the way through to the point where it again emerged into the day. There were spacious chambers hollowed out of the rock, intersecting and leading into one another; and superiority of numbers would avail but little, unless they could come upon their man by surprise, or bolt him into a judicious ambush at some one point.

The sergeant had been a sportsman in his day, and done some stalking of wild game, to say nothing of illicit stills, and, therefore, he advanced to reconnoitre, leaving the remainder of the party huddled in a heap behind a boulder of projecting rock. The interval of his absence was passed in excited whispers, and examination of firelocks; and any casual observer might have been rather startled in this wild rocky spot, to see five dark figures thus crouching in concealment, and another creeping from point to point a short distance in advance, with bare and cautious head.

The time seemed long, and it *was* long before he returned again; but the warmly satisfied expression on his face kindled corresponding hopes at once in his followers' breasts. The greatest piece of good fortune, he said. He had seen him. The position was most favourable : just beyond the entrance to the principal cave his hat could be detected above the dim rocks inside, and if they could only approach without his hearing them—if by good chance he should only happen to be asleep—they could be down upon him in a body, and secure him without trouble. Still in case of accidents, two of them had better be posted at the further entrance, and two were accordingly sent round for that purpose. After giving them time to get to their posts, the remaining force, under the sergeant's lead, cocked their pieces, and stealthily advanced by the way he had planned as he came along. It was an exciting progress, and they almost held their breaths for fear a sound should reach him, knowing the sensitiveness of such men's consciences and hearing. One of them, as luck would have it, detaches a loosened stone, and it rattles down the path with an agonizing noise. The sergeant halts at once, and looks round fiercely, and for some moments they all crouch down in petrified silence to await the result, or to let the alarm pass off. Many minutes pass, and hope revives again.

Motioning then for perfect silence, their leader cautiously proceeds once more, and one by one, in single file, they follow—halting when he halts, moving on when he moves on—fully expecting, after that unlucky accident, to see their quarry appear above them somewhere reconnoitring. Even the presence of each other doesn't prevent them altogether from an uncomfortable feeling of the lonely wildness of the place, and a certain imaginative consciousness of the character of the crime which was lurking in the midst of it, and so close to them. Every moment they feel brings them nearer to a blood-guilty fugitive, and there is a kind of vague impressiveness and awe about the thought, which only the leader of the party was entirely exempt from. He had quite enough to occupy his thoughts in the precautionary strained attention required to ensure success.

Only a short hundred yards now separate them

from the entrance to the cave, and a further exploration is necessary, before emerging from behind the intervening rocks. Again, therefore, they halt, while the sergeant makes a downward detour to find out the exact point they have to make for, and to see how obstacles are to be avoided. With bated breath and halting step he makes his way from rock to rock until the broken opening into the inner darkness comes partially into view, and then he suddenly ducks down behind a stone, as he finds when his eyes become more searching in the dark dimness of the cave, now close in front, that he must have been for a good half minute in full view of the occupant; unless he was, as he scarcely dared to hope, asleep.

The sudden discovery gave him quite a turn, to use an expressive, if inelegant, phrase, and he waited in anxious suspense for some minutes before venturing to peer cautiously out again to see whether the prize was still there. It was, and still in the same position apparently; and further observation detected more than had appeared before —the muzzles of two horse pistols pointing to the light. If he was to wake, the sergeant couldn't but confess that his capture might be an ugly business now, and at one moment thought of disabling him with a shot as he lay. That idea, however, was very soon scouted, and after laying out their line of approach, he picked his way back to his comrades, carefully keeping out of sight this time, and informed them in a whisper how the land lay, and what, in all probability, there would be to encounter. As the constable was the biggest and strongest man of the four, the sergeant thought it might be advisable that he should head the party and grapple with the ruffian at the first surprise. The constable, however, thought that as the sergeant had led the way so far, and knew exactly the route which they had to take, it would be better that he should keep the lead, and if he should unluckily be shot, there would still be three behind to back him up. The other younger members of the force not volunteering for the front, the sergeant braced up his nerves to take all the glory of the danger on himself. It was arranged, however, that as far as possible, when they once broke cover, it should be in one united rush, which would take the unconscious victim by surprise, and allow them to overpower him before he had the presence of mind to fire. Other details having been agreed upon they set out once more with redoubled caution, pausing at every step, the slightest grating of their boots against the rock causing an impatient thrill, and making them grasp their firelocks, and set their teeth angrily to the tension of their excited nerves. At last the moment of the final halt arrived: they were close to the corner, where the dank grass and bits of stunted shrubs hung over the entrance to the cave. On the other side of the projecting rock before them, just a short way in, was the man who had baffled all their efforts hitherto, now within their reach. What if he should appear outside while they stood there?

A few moments were allowed for recovering breath and getting rid, as far as possible, of superfluous excitement, and then the sergeant instructing them to keep close beside him, asks, "Are you ready?" waits one second or two more, and then with a whispered "Now!" dashes round the corner, closely followed by the other three, and a moment after, without a shot fired, has grasped triumphantly an old, old hat, and a pair of good, stout, cabbage-stalks!

Alas! poor sergeant!

What a damper upon the energy of the force! They look at each other in savage disappointment; with much the same feelings as a stealthy poacher may experience in the evening dusk when he finds that he has expended upon a careless irresponsive tuft of fern the cautious shot which he had intended for what seemed a most undoubted hare.

It was very trying, certainly; but it did so happen that the preparers of this little surprise had been very much more nearly promoting the wanted man's arrest than they supposed. Unknown to them, Terence Mc Gowan had returned to the neighbourhood the previous evening, to take one final look at the little place and house which held his all upon the earth, before making his way to Galway to take the passage which had been secured for him in an emigrant ship to America.

Kathleen, he heard to his disappointment, had been removed to Mount-Stewart with her children, weak and ill, but recovering; and his mother had been taken in by a neighbour on the roadside, and was going to become a dealing woman—*i.e.* a dispenser, for equivalent remuneration, of tea and sugar, and such like commodities on a very small scale. Still he must see the place, even though its spirit might be fled; and, as he had often done at night before, when Kathleen was raving in delirium all unconscious of his neighbourhood, he crept down the mountain after nightfall into the birch-wood at the back, and waiting till all sounds upon the road had ceased, and he seemed alone with the starry stillness of the night, emerged upon the well-known pasture cautiously and creepingly—he had almost become accustomed to this shame-faced, sneaking, unmanly, cowering kind of life now—and slowly drew across it to the deserted building which was once his home, her home, and his children's home—now, pointed at by passers-by as the place where Terence Mc Gowan the murderer used to live.

Was it worth while, he asked himself again, as he had asked himself a hundred times before, to sacrifice all joy in life, which they might have had elsewhere, for one moment's gratification of a poor and barren revenge, which left him not one whit the better afterwards? Better, indeed! he thought, bitterly, as he looked in through the window at the cold ashes on the hearth, and the sinking despondency of his heart told him but too emphatically how much worse. If they *had* been turned out of everything, he had the strength, and energy of a man, and a clear conscience; and, though the parting would have been a grief, what was it to the haunting inward dread which now accompanied him in all his movements? If it *was* injustice, could such revenge be justified? He shuddered at himself and turned away; and as he passed the fastened door, where Kathleen used to sit and watch him in the fields in summer time, he saw a notice posted on it, and, reading with some difficulty, found it was a warning to any man who thought to take that farm that he would do it at his peril. He tore it down impatiently, and turned towards the grey deserted pile across the glen, beyond which the trees were darkly feathered against the yellow glory of the rising moon, which was bathing the mountains in a flood of beauty, far too pure for him; and then unconsciously his eyes sought the fatal spot within the wood, and as quickly were averted from it to the grandeur of that full-orbed majesty growing up the sky with a stately pure magnificence that made him doubly feel how mean and vile a creature of the earth he was. Such scene was not for him, and in the growing light not venturing a further stay, he bent his steps once more towards the height; taking thence one farewell look upon it all, passed down into the shade beyond, and traversed many a mile of moor until he reached the high boundary of the wood above Glen Annagh's gleaming waters.

The night was passed under the coldly shining silver moon, upon a rough heather bed on the outskirts of the wood; and the short day was already two hours gone before he woke from the heavy sleep of bodily fatigue into the damp consciousness of a dull grey world. Travelling in daylight was dangerous, as a rule, but in this unfrequented part less caution seemed required. Accordingly, after breakfasting off a lump of bread, the remains of yesterday's provision, and drinking a draught of water from a neighbouring spring, which he had often drank happier and purer draughts from in other days, he plunged into the long deep wood; and unable to resist one passing look at the spot where he had sat with Kathleen on that sweet May Sunday when she agreed to give up all the world for him, he bent his steps in that direction, and stood once more upon the shore.

It was a very different scene that he now gazed upon—as different as was his own life, now clouded and dark with despondency and remorse, to what it then was, basking in the soft light of love and hope. There was a still stagnation in the air; the rocks about the leafless islands lay dark and black upon the leaden water; the white walls of the chapel on the mountain opposite looked desolate and bare; the smoke from burning weeds was rising straight and lifeless to the lowering banks of clouds which sullenly hung like a gloomy pall all down the mountain sides; there was a sound of dripping in the trees, a damp, depressing sound; and as the scared wild duck quacked away into the silence, leaving a broad disturbance in its wake upon the motionless water, or a chance curlew shrieked a melancholy passing note, to make the desolation seem more desolate, there scarcely could have been a greater contrast, Terence thought, as he recalled the perfect loveliness of that May-day of love. Old Thady's house was visible in the distance from where he stood, and the thought of what his pride and all her family must have suffered from his connection, now added another drop of gall to the bitterness of remorse.

Brooding thus, the minutes slipped by. He had sat down to try and live again for, at all events, a few short moments in the past; but the shadow of the present fell upon it all, and gloom, and ever-deepening gloom, was everywhere shutting out all pleasant pictures of past joys, and abstracting thought into itself, until activity was roused again with a sudden start at the sound of voices through the wood—men's voices, coming, too, towards him. In a moment he was on his feet, looking round for flight along the shore, a rocky shore—or through the wood; no path. There was no time to stand thinking. The steps, and there were many of them, were rapidly approaching, and he had scarcely concealed himself behind a cluster of somewhat larger rocks a short distance on, when a party of six policemen came out of the wood on to the green above, talking, as he could hear, about himself. One of them took advantage of the opening to the shore to come and get a drink, and came straight to the very spot where Terence had been sitting a minute or two before. Having satisfied his thirst, he turned to follow the others, and his eye fell upon the marks of recent footsteps in the moss.

"That's queer!" he exclaimed, confining his remark to himself only as audience: barring, of course, Terence, who was not twenty yards off, lying flat on his back among the stones, partially concealed by the corpse of a *ci-devant* larch.

"Hi, sergeant! hallo!" the policeman cried, after a moment's further investigation; and Terence thought it was all over with him, and began to calculate the possibility of escaping by the rocks. He was as good a runner, he thought, as any of these men, who, from the voice of the thirsty one, he knew to be from Geraldsbridge; but he heard this man lay down his musket against a stone, and if they were loaded, which they probably were, he might as well give in.

It should not be without a struggle, though. The gallows—a gaping crowd beneath! That one last shame, at least, he never would submit to.

The sergeant's reply came back from within the wood some little distance on, too far to shout an explanation sufficient to bring him back, and the discoverer moves towards him where he stands to communicate the fact of footmarks on the shore. After a little parley the whole party comes talking back, the sergeant in no humour to be convinced, and still very sore about the hoax from which they were then returning.

"Why, it's your own, stupid!" was his first exclamation.

"No, no, not those; these here," said the other. "They're not as fresh now; and there's a mark of where, I'll be sworn, some person was sitting not five minutes since."

"Psha!" rejoined the sergeant; "it's where ducks were paddling, and there's where they left the water. See the drip of them on the stones!"

"That's a drip I made myself in drinking," said the Crusoe of the discovery; "and that's ne'er a duck's mark, I'll hold ye!" pointing to the fading impression of what certainly had very much the appearance of a boot.

The other examined it, and some said one thing and some another; and Terence, in a fever of suspense, heard every word they said, and though a pointed stone was under the very middle of his back, dared not stir an inch to better the position.

It was suggested then that they should search the covert round.

"And what for?" asked their leader. "Is it another wild goose chase you're for? you haven't had enough, maybe, for one morning. If it was a man that was there at all, is it here he'd be now, if it was the man we're after? Do you think he'd wait for us, when he heard us coming?"

"He couldn't go far, any way, and him sitting there so recent, wherever he'd be," said another.

"Come along, men!" said the sergeant authoritatively. "We'll waste no more time. The man we want's in America, I tell you, and I'll not believe any person that'll deny it. Any other that might have been out here makes no matter, for all we're concerned, and we'll not be bothering ourselves looking after him."

Against this decision there was no appeal, and the voices and heavy policeman tread died away into the wood, and left Terence with a most intense feeling of relief, both bodily and mental.

After giving a few moments to congratulating himself on another hair-breadth escape, he dived into the thicket, and was in full flight once more.

CHAPTER XIII.

IN a trellised, rose-twined cottage, in a sunny nook of the park at Mount-Stewart, lay Kathleen, a beautiful wan shadow—her dark black eyes the homes of a silent, unchanging melancholy, which deepened only (as far as she had strength to feel degrees of any heart-emotion) when her children came about her, with their tiny wondering looks, and pleaded for caresses which she had no power to give. Nora used to pay her daily visits, and Lady Mountstewart overflowed with a sympathy and kindness which Kathleen could only return by grateful looks, so sweetly sad in presence of the one thought which occupied her shadowy life, that that kind old lady declared that, in all the pictures she had ever seen, she never had found such pathetic beauty; perhaps because painted pathos, idealized beyond conception,

—if that were not a paradox—can never stir the compassionate and sympathetic thrill which a lesser flesh-and-blood reality evokes.

Her husband's name was never mentioned. Once, and once only, she had asked about him, and they had told her that he had left the country. She closed her eyes, and had never spoken of him since, although imagination never left the subject idle,— accompanying him in all his wanderings, all his hardships, all his fears, and even conjuring up his presence in the still lonely hours of the night, when the moonbeams streamed across the room, and made it seem a spirit-world of light. So powerful was the influence of these imaginative feelings that she fainted with a sudden scream one night on opening her eyes to the lattice window, and seeing, as she afterwards averred, a figure standing in the moonlight just outside—the figure of her husband, gazing, in a fixed melancholy attitude, straight towards the bed on which she lay; so changed, but still her husband, watching her as she slept, it seemed; and she never could be persuaded that her fancy had deceived her, only smiled, and felt, however it might be explained, that she was right.

It happened the night after this fright of Kathleen's, the cause of which she told to no one for long weeks after, that Shirley was returning by the last train which reached Newtown Mount-Stewart towards midnight, freighted with emigrants on their way to Galway. The station-master had stepped up to speak to him as he left the train, and while they were talking, a strong, powerful-looking man, with a slouched hat and a six weeks' beard, came out under the lamp on to the platform where they were standing, evidently in great distress of mind. After looking at Shirley, whose back was turned to him, he walked rapidly up to where the porter and two countrymen, who had arrived by the train, were waiting until a truck had been attached and the noisy cargo had moved on, and begged them to assist him to get as far as Galway: his passage was taken by the next vessel, he was a shilling or two short of the fare, and he could not get a ticket—would they take pity on him? "Here," he exclaimed, "that's all I have in the world," rummaging out a knife, an old pipe, a tobacco-box—"No, not that," putting back what looked like a lock of hair. "Won't one o' you take them from me? Have pity, for God's sake, and don't let the train be goin' on without me!"

His dramatic distress, and the agony of mind he was in impressed the compassionate hearts of his countrymen at once, and they were telling him to put back his dudeen and wee box again, while they got their money out, when Shirley, who had been passing and heard the last few words, stopped and asked the porter what the matter was.

"It's a poor fellow, my lord, that hasn't the price of his ticket, and that has his passage taken to America by this next ship. But, please God, he'll have it now."

"Here, let me give it to him," said Shirley. "I can afford it better than you, I dare say. How much is it you want?"

At the first sound of Shirley's voice, and hearing him addressed as my lord, the man had started and become suddenly subdued, and now, as he answered, he seemed ashamed to take the money, and kept his face in shadow while he did so with an uneasy manner which Shirley attributed to wounded pride; perhaps he would rather have been assisted by the others.

The train began to move, and Shirley called to the station-master to stop it, while this man got his ticket; watching him as he passed under the lamp again with the satisfactory feeling of having made a good use of a few shillings, and a certain dim feeling that, in other garb and circumstances, he must have seen that man before. He passed him again taking his ticket, but the other was too absorbed in watching the station-master putting it through its stamping to look up or notice who was passing, and a few moments after the train had borne him away with its living freight, and the lurid gleam of the engine smoke was disappearing down the darkness of the line.

Shirley mounted his dog-cart and drove off towards home, and the incident very soon was forgotten. The two countrymen watched the train out of sight, and as they left the station behind, one whispered under his breath to the other:

"Whisht, Paddy, do you know who that poor fellow was?—It was TERENCE Mc GOWAN."

The other started and half stood still, and then they walked on for some time in silence.

You know, of course, that it *was* Terence Mc Gowan ; and you have guessed by this time that in his anxiety to see the place at least where Kathleen was, if not herself, he had risked a visit to the neighbourhood of Mount-Stewart, and so spent the time which he ought to have allowed for travelling across country to the coast, until he found it necessary to resort to such a *tour de force* as he has just survived.

If Shirley was ever to know that he had been instrumental to his escape in this way, he might, perhaps, be glad on private grounds that it had not fallen to him to bring Kathleen's husband to justice. But seeing that it is only in this very present year of 1870 that the occurrence happened, it is not easy to say what the future may bring forth in the way of information. At any rate he had not heard of it before the vessel started; and Terence mixed in with the other emigrants without detection, notwithstanding the vigilance of the police.

The last embraces on the shore were over. The harsh tones of the final bell are ringing out amidst the confusion of wild laments which fills the air. The side of the vessel is crowded with tearful faces stretching out their arms in a farewell agony to the friends they leave behind them on the quay, and amid wailing and crying and tears and gesticulations of grief on every side, the good ship slowly moves away—slowly and surely from friends and relatives and country to an unknown future over miles and miles of never-ending sea.

Gloomy and apart the murderer looks upon the scene. No sorrowing friends had come to see him off into a hopeful future where hardship and privation were to be unknown. A cheerless prospect was opening from a dark past, and the sense of relief which he felt as the vessel cleared the harbour mouth and seemed to leave detection on the shore behind was short-lived before the bitter pang of parting from his country, and the longing thought of the little spot among the hills where the joys of industry and innocence had once been known, and never would be more. The white-dotted town merged dimly into haze, the mountains sank below the line, and Ireland faded out of sight. But though other straining eyes might dry their tears, and others' sobs might cease, and other thoughts be turned with hopeful looks towards the west, there was no such cessation of regret, no such mitigation of the longing agony of home and country which Terence felt.

He had escaped, and that was all. When next we hear of him, it possibly will be as Captain Mc Gowan of the Fenian army.

APPENDIX.

APPENDIX.

(1)

Vol. I.—p. 171.

REALITIES of Irish life appear to have an interest for the reading public, and therefore I may mention a pertinent illustration of this particular feature of the Irish character, which might have been witnessed here the other day. A good-looking, almost gentlemanlike boy, of twenty, or thereabouts, had been arrested for cattle-stealing, and brought before my brother, in his magisterial capacity, to answer to the charge. At the time I saw him he had pleaded guilty, and while the warrant for his committal was being made out, was standing handcuffed between two constables, with an old father and mother beside him, in a most pathetic misery of shame and tears. It was the most touching little drama I ever saw. One generally does one's pathos on the stage or in books; but a bit of real nature such as this was, so rare to see, is worth all the books or plays that ever were written. The mother, bowed down with shame, wringing her hands in a silent agony, far too deep for sympathy to reach; the old man, in his crumpled hat and torn blue coat, with the tears running down his wrinkled face, moving restlessly to and fro, as if anxious to escape from possible observation, and yet returning again at intervals to look into the boy's face with a silent reproachful misery, which was more than he could bear; and the handcuffed hands had to be raised more than once to brush away the trickling tear which overflowed in spite of him: even the constables, who ought to be inured to scenes of the kind, shifted their positions uneasily, and seemed to wish that the interview was over. For seven generations, the old father told me afterwards, when I met them wearily trudging

APPENDIX. 259

up the mountain to their cabin-home, after seeing the last of their boy—for seven generations, he said, his lips quivering, and the tears swelling into his eyes again, such a thing had not happened in his family; and the neighbours all could vouch for the truth of what he said: it would be as good for them now leave the country altogether.

(2)

Vol. I.—p. 250.

THE Special Commissioner of *The Times* is a very fair specimen of the reliability of many prominent authors of recent literature on Ireland. If his rhetoric was to be trusted the Irish tenant would be the most miserable creature in the universe, and his life perfectly insupportable under the accumulated consciousness of insecurity which his friends have piled upon him. But is a writer to be trusted who leaves the more congenial atmosphere of the Dublin law courts to announce to Irish landowners, through the columns of *The Times*, that "it is a silly fallacy to suppose that the Irishman is idle?" Who further declares that the Irish farmer "readily takes to an improved method of agriculture?" and who (still serious apparently) asserts —of course from a long practical acquaintance with the idiosyncrasies of the Irish tenant—that it is " a most mischievous and stupid delusion " to suppose that he is unreasonable in respect of covenants? These were sufficiently startling facts to have been able to collect almost at the outset of his tour. But when the same writer goes on to state that in the Queen's County there has not been a lease given for twenty years, and a Queen's County landlord writes next day to say that, within the last seven years, he has given some five-and-forty, and would have given more if his tenants had cared to have them; why, to one unversed in the arts of special correspondence, there seemed to be something so almost irreconcilable in the two statements, that one's faith in the oracle who was going to tell us all about it, was of necessity somewhat dashed. Since that, however, the clue to his letters has been furnished from an authentic source. Upon being asked by a noble lord, who was driving him about his property, whether he was sure that some statements, which he was taking down at the moment from a third party, were facts, or only mere hearsay, he turned round at once with the astonishing rejoinder,—"Oh! I take all the information I can get, hearsay or not." It's a pity that Mr. Gladstone could not have known this; and then, perhaps, he would not have framed his introductory speech so manifestly upon the information conveyed in these letters.

Now, without in the least pretending to lay any sort of claim to infallibility for one's own utterances, and deprecating the imputation of any such pretension, one may fairly protest against the acceptance of such an authority, and reasonably resent the arrogant and dictatorial tone in which he measured out his justice to the landlords of the country. Fluency, of course, is a very desirable gift; and descriptive power a great enjoyment apparently—though some people may think that the pages of a guide-book would have been more suitable for its display—and it may be a great thing to have Arthur Young's experience of the last century at one's fingers' ends; but surely some other qualifications than these are required for writing upon such a subject as Irish land; and it is just these necessary qualifications which, it is generally admitted throughout Ireland, were not possessed by the fluent gentleman in question. His discussion, for instance, of the Ulster Tenant Right, through long columns of smoothly flowing periods, followed up, as he was leaving that part of the country, by an admission (which was certainly not required for Irish readers) that he really knew very little about it, was scarcely respectful to his employers, and rather insulting to the public. Starting with a preconceived prejudice in favour of a general system of leases, every statement or misstatement which could further that opinion was put prominently forward, and it was only when he came to the small holdings of Kerry, and found that Tipperary and the Midland plains did not constitute the whole of Ireland, and perhaps because he found that *The Times* itself was not supporting him, that he was obliged to modify, to some extent, his original opinions. From that time he dealt more with facts, or what purported to be facts, and concluded what was virtually the last of the series of exercises, in the following oracular words :—

"As regards the whole system of ownership in Ireland, unsound as it is in too many places, it is obvious that any change in it must be in the strictest sense voluntary, and most fully respect the rights of property; such a change must be gradual and partial, and can only be thought of as supplemental in any settlement of the land question; yet it may be the duty of real statesmanship, on grounds of high political expediency, to afford facilities for this consummation."

It will be seen at once from this what the gentleman's ultimate views upon the subject were, and it is almost a pity that this effective farewell should have been spoilt by the subsequent appearance of more last words.

But it is not only from random journalists that the country has been suffering. Busy pamphleteers have been hard at work, as even English people know to their cost, and their carefully collected misstatements have generally escaped the exposure which happily fell to the lot of Mr. Samuelson, M.P. It was an unkind return for his Quixotic indignation on behalf of a tenantry in Westmeath, that they should turn round upon him unanimously and protest against the interference of "this English manufacturing gentleman" between themselves and their agent, with whom they had always been on the best of terms. Such conduct must have seemed almost like ingratitude to their would-be benefactor.

Mr. Charles Buxton, on the other hand, is an actual owner of property in Ireland, bought up cheap after the famine, on purely philanthropic motives as we are told, and therefore he writes with some authority. From him we find that the panacea, as exemplified in his own practice, for giving to Irish tenants the security they desire, is to import a Scotch farmer into their place, and give him a lease. His experience will be valuable in Committee.

(3)

Vol. II.—p. 25.

SCOTCHMEN are wont to assert that there is no country where the desire for education and learning is so strong as in their own. Ireland, however, may fairly claim an equality in this respect. In Scotland, perhaps, next to Prussia, there *is* more education: but, as was remarked somewhere the other day, it is the end of religion which education serves, rather than the love of learning for its own sake, which makes, or made them originally enthusiastic in the cause. It is not a national instinct as it is in Ireland. Knox raised the plant in the hot-house of religious zeal, and it thrives now, in part, owing to the continuance of the same artificial heat. In Ireland, there never was such a motive cause, or such a moving agent for the diffusion of education; and yet there has always been a greed for it through the country. Go back to the old days of Brehons and harpers, and Tanists, and you find that, notwithstanding their free roving savage kind of life, learning was by no means despised. The same want called into existence the old hedge schoolmasters, who taught their schools in the open air, for want of building accommodation, and who found sedition and pedantry a very paying combination. In the present day the poorest man tries to put together a decent suit of patches for his children to go turn about to the National School in; and a bright scholar is always an object of interest in the neighbourhood, and a subject of boasting to his family. The announcement of a holiday in an Irish school is received without any gratitude whatever; and the peasantry have such an aversion to the idea of their children growing up dunces, that Cardinal Cullen will probably not attempt to gratify his denominational prejudices, by carrying out his threat of forbidding the sacraments of the Church to parents who allow their children to attend the National Schools. Even his assumption of the land question into his dictatorial programme will hardly bolster up his authority among the people, if he tries to force them into ignorance. Considering the opposition of the priests, whose interest of course it is that there should be as little reason as possible for authority to overcome, and the various antagonistic causes of poverty and religious distinctions, which hinder education as well as every other development of the country, it points to the existence of a decided intellectual need which insists upon finding sustenance, that there should be so much intelligence and knowledge found amongst the lower orders in Ireland. One is often surprised in the Highlands of Scotland, to find how much information is to be obtained from the gillies and keepers one comes in contact with; but within the last few months, in this very wild neighbourhood of Leitrim, I have heard a boatman discussing Sir Walter Scott and his novels; have received a poetic effusion from a mute inglorious Burns (and there are many such scattered about), whose education had been confined to the study of the English Grammar, and a spelling-book or two, with an old dictionary for light reading, but whose thoughts nevertheless run into rhyme as he cuts rushes on the mountain side; and I have been applied to by a youth of tattered appearance, and seventeen years (on the reputation, I suppose, of having been to Cambridge College), to examine him in the first six books of Euclid, Algebra up to Quadratic Equations, and various other long-forgotten horrors of a like nature, in order that his fitness for the assistant-mastership of a neighbouring National School might be vouched for to the patron of the same. The idea of being called upon to set a paper in algebra up to quadratics, and to talk about the Binomial Theorem, as if one knew all about it, and was in daily communication, in fact, some years after taking a *classical* degree! On the sixth book of Euclid he had moreover a book of "exercises;" but he was not pressed to bring it. Here was a boy, however, who had educated himself up to this point, with merely a foundation from a learned uncle in another cabin.

Then to continue — not to mention talking philology with Bartley McLoughlin above—(why should Scotland, by the way, have a professor of Gaelic anymore than Ireland a professor of Irish?) I have even been lost in political economy with an old labourer, the sleeves of whose coat were two grey stockings with the feet cut off, who couldn't read, and who yet asserted that in his opinion the labouring man was the least "justified" of any class in the kingdom; that he got less consideration; seldom a bit of flesh meat; that his wages were always the same, no matter whether he might be throwing up dirt out of the ditch, or what he might be doing; and when it was through him only that the country got food to eat, he thought they ought not to be treated as they were. It was a happy coincidental illustration of the common liability to admitted error of tutored and untutored minds, that I should chance that same evening to come across the following passage in Mr. Thornton's book upon labour:—"It is so natural," he says, " to think that what is, and always has been, is right, and ought always to endure, that to most of us it never occurs to question the propriety of a division of labour, which devolves upon two-thirds of the community the whole duty of supporting, and leaves the other third with comparatively little to do but to be supported."

Compared with the agricultural labourer in many parts of England, though that to be sure is not a very high standard of comparison, the Irish labourer is well off. He is content with less; he likes dirt, and dirt is cheap. In the poorer districts he has fuel at his door almost, failing him only in wet seasons. He has never been accustomed to meat, and therefore he doesn't feel the want of it. He often has a patch of potato ground along with his house—that is, a professed labourer ; very many, of course, are the superfluous sons of small tenants who live at home,—and not seldom a cow; and if he gets a little dripping or bacon, or fatty substance of that kind "to grease a bit of cabbage" for his dinner, he enjoys the rise from potatoes as much as the country parson does his flight from boiled mutton to the great man's *entrées*. He rarely gets less than a shilling a day—in the far west I believe tenpence is the pay—and if not regularly employed, or working out through the country, he will "get his support"—the run of his teeth, that is to say, as well : and unless he is much more given to far-sighted reasoning than the rest of his countrymen, he will hardly acknowledge that the Government Land Bill has definitely improved his condition.

(4)

Vol. II.—p. 39.

It was a rather singular coincidence that the night after writing this chapter, the Banshee itself or herself, or whatever self it may profess, should do me the honour of an express howl. If it had been the night before I might have thought that imagination, having been worked up to excitement-pitch by the nature of the subject upon which it was engaged, had attempted to supplement its fiction by a fancied reality. But it was not the night before, it was the night after, towards twelve o'clock, and I was sitting of course before a fire that was burning low, deep in one of the *Saturday Review's* most bitterly unimaginative articles, when I was suddenly startled by a noise like the crying of a child from the bank of the stream, not half a dozen yards from the window. At the time I didn't know that the Banshee was supposed to cry like a child, and had represented it as having a woman's voice, so that the idea never occurred to me. But as I happened to be quite alone, without a creature but a double-barrelled gun in the house, and no other human being within call, it *was* startling to hear a child crying close outside one's window at midnight. At first I thought, by the mournful pettish kind of tone, that it must have lost its way; then that it was being murdered, and it struck me as a very indecent joke to play at one's door; then it occurred to me that it might be some tumbler's decoy, and as the night was very dark, and there were a good many shrubs about, I didn't go out— if it *was* a murder, discretion suggested that it would keep very well till morning. All this time the same mournful wail went on, varied once by a noise that sounded like strangling, and then it flitted round to the front of the house and ceased for a time; and then commenced again further off, and floated weirdly away upon the night. Very odd, I thought, resuming my paper again; evidently not a murder, or a locomotive one, if it was; must be a child gone astray, as it had turned in the direction of the high-road eventually; though, why it should be out at that time of night I couldn't pretend to conjecture. I finished my article, went to bed, didn't wake up in the night screaming, and inquired next day if anybody had been talking of a missing child. "Oh!" they said at once; "it must have been the Banshee you heard; she'll often be found crying down about that cottage; and there's very few in the country 'll leave the place by that gate after night." "And was there no person in the house but yourself when she riz the cry?" one old woman asked. "Ah, *now*! I wouldn't have liked to hear it at all then,"* she continued, when she found that I had been alone, and looking at me with a kind of awful interest, she proceeded to relate various reminiscences on the subject, accumulated through a long and superstitious life. There was an old man lying dead at the time at the other end of the place, and it was conjectured, for my comfort, that it might be for him she was crying; but why she should wander away a mile or more from his corpse to give me a benefit

* In Irish they have a very cheerful name for the Banshee — yellow maggot.

on the head of it I couldn't understand, and therefore wouldn't admit the explanation. A small nephew up at the house happening to be ill with a cold at the time, most particular inquiries were made after his health for some days after, always followed up by an intimation that the inquirer had been told that the Banshee had been heard crying about my cottage. Indeed, my Banshee bred and multiplied in a most astonishingly rapid manner, and was heard after that all down about the lake and through the wild woods along the shore, wailing and shrieking in a most supernatural and owl-like manner every night. As to my own experience, not being much given to supernatural beliefs, I am inclined to think from subtle indications of a natural solution, which I could afterwards recall, that it was nothing after all but a cat with a stomach-ache. I confess I never heard such tones from a cat before. But there had been poison laid about the house not many days previously, and that might account, perhaps, for the phenomenon of tone, or delusion of apprehension, if you like. I never heard it since, and must only conclude, therefore, that the poor animal has passed away.

But though not much affecting superstitious terrors, I don't mind saying that I should have been very sorry to live alone at night, as I was at that time, in a solitary cottage by the wood, in burglarious England. Here I have not the slightest fear: and though they tell me there ought to be, there is not even a shutter to the windows at present. Of course when writing about murders in the dead of night, one hears footsteps outside the window, and naturally peers into the kitchen to see if any one is there before going to bed. But one might do the same over Miss Braddon in the securest house in the country. Perhaps if I had been a landlord I should not have cared to show such implicit confidence in the people; and I dare say I should not have chosen to do so *in propriâ personâ*, if it had not been for the priest's interference with my housekeeper's sleeping arrangements. But we are not sufficiently educated in Ireland as yet to have acquired a taste for the fine arts of robbery and burglary; and a man told me the other day that it would be a very forward kind of a chap that would offer to come near a house with a gun in it.

(5)

Vol. II.—p. 50.

I HAVE been unfortunate, I suppose, in my experience of exemplary Irish clergymen, who are supposed to be such godsends of cultivation and piety to their neighbourhoods; and I am also unfortunate, I suppose, in having a sad failing for truth, for I could point out at this moment a specimen of a church district, where, within a radius of a dozen miles or so, might be found one clergyman with an illegitimate son; another, and more than another, who had no duty but fishing in the summer months, and preparations for the same arduous sport during the winter season; another, who was as fond of his tumbler of punch as the priest himself; another, with some three hundred souls valued at five pound a head, who is gay; and another, an imported Methodist, not of college extraction, who can hardly be credited with much refining influence, but whose antecedents have imbued him at least with something of the religious zeal which orthodoxy, as a rule, repudiates. Illiterate clergymen are not more numerous in Ireland, perhaps, than they are in England.

These facts are mentioned for the comfort of such good people as may have felt qualms of conscience about giving their vote for the disestablishment of the Irish Church.

---

(6)

Vol. II.—p. 98.

THIS dependence upon each other's opinion, and fear of ridicule, is one of the most powerful levers which the priest has for moving the individuals of his flock in any direction he desires, and he uses it on every sort of occasion, in season and out of season. It is never more out of season— perhaps, than at a funeral, when he sends a hat round among the friends and relations of the dead man, and calls out in a loud voice what each man gives. "On a big corpse," he will sometimes take as much as five-and-twenty, or thirty pounds.

(7)

Vol. II.—p. 128.

THIS was an actual case, quoted by me in a letter to *The Times*, in December last. It is an exceptional one, but not very exceptional, and it cannot be too clearly understood that tenant-right so called in Ulster, has no analogy with tenant-right proper, such as exists in Lincolnshire. Tenant-right in Ulster means merely the good-will, the privilege of occupation undisturbed by the bullets of the out-goer's friends.

(8)

Vol. II.—p. 149.

IT is a common thing to hear the Government excused for the impunity which they permit to murderers in Ireland, on the plea that it is impossible to do anything where there is no public opinion in the country—where the sympathy of the people is all on the side of the murderer. It is nothing of the kind. Murder has no such attractions for the majority of Irishmen; but they are very keenly alive to fear. In the case of agrarian murders, there is, of course, a certain sympathy in some exceptional cases; but the undetected murders are not by any means all agrarian; and even where they are, what prevents men coming forward to give evidence is much more the prevailing terrorism, which has been stamped upon the country by a few energetic and unscrupulous ruffians, whose organization the Government countenances by suffering it to exist. From the original Ribbon nucleus, a great upas-tree of fear (to borrow the Prime Minister's expressive simile) has overshadowed the country; and perhaps when the Government has finished lopping off the branches of the one they are at present engaged upon, they may think this one worth their attention also: although, to be sure, the loyal and peaceable part of the population not having given much trouble, can very well wait for their share of the justice which is now being dispensed. In the meanwhile, nobody dares come forward to give evidence against his neighbour for any crime whatever, no matter how nearly he himself may be affected by it. Three or four years ago, some six or seven men beat a fellow-workman to death outside my mother's gate, in a midland county —Westmeath—because he was supposed to have given information of some improper practices which were being carried on inside the place. Four or five were arrested, but no evidence was forthcoming, and they had to be set at liberty again. We all knew perfectly well who the principal men implicated were, and so of course did every one about the neighbourhood; but no one would come forward to give evidence, and there has, of course, been no conviction. Was that sympathy with the murderers? when a man could never be sure but what another who was working next to him was engaged to beat his brains out as he went home that evening. Was he likely to have any sympathy with outrages of the kind, or likely to rejoice at the impunity which rendered his own life not worth a moment's purchase perhaps? All over Ireland, if you begin to talk to a man about Ribbonism he becomes reserved at once, and shrinks into himself with the consciousness of that secret overshadowing terror which has been allowed to spread through the country unchecked.

While the above has been going through the press my mother has added one more to the list of victims which the present Government may claim for their message-of-peace policy—that policy of permissive apathy which is rapidly emptying the country of the few proprietors who still managed to live with some sense of security upon their properties. Because, forsooth, she declined to discharge her steward at the dictation of some person, or persons, to whom he had become obnoxious, it was intimated to her that she was next on the list; and while delicately reminded of the year '45, when her brother was mutilated on the same spot, she was informed that both herself and the steward would before long be shot. Every workman about the place was discharged until the writers of the letters were given up—which, of course, they never will be—the house is shut up, and my mother is now abroad. It was very truly said in one of the letters in question, "the times are gone by when yous could do as you liked;" they have, indeed—ruffianism is now supreme. Ireland is henceforth to be governed according to Irish ideas. Law is not popular amongst the riotous section of Irishmen which is taken to represent Ireland; and, therefore, law is henceforth not to be enforced. The Prime Minister has no sympathy whatever with the orderly classes, and virtually tells them from his place in Parliament, that, owing to the defective legislation of the last century, they deserve to be shot. This may be so. But here was no question of land. What justification will he find for the assumption of dictatorial rights, to be maintained by murder, by the employed over his employer? There was no hint of injustice or harshness, the employer in question being liberal and benevolent to a fault in all her dealings with dependents, and having left in this part of the country a name that is regarded with the most extravagant devotion. Upon what strange plea are we to make allowances for the permission of such dictation? The same Minister can find it in his conscience to deplore the absenteeism from which Ireland suffers; and his Government is asked by some in Ireland to stultify itself by putting a tax on an evil which it is itself, if not creating, at least increasing and maintaining. "Order, security, and peace once threatened," M. Ollivier said, in the French Chamber a short time ago, "and liberty is lost." Who would live in a country where there was no liberty, if he could help himself? And how could any man be taxed for going elsewhere to look for what every one has a right to expect in his own country, and which he did not find there? One would have thought that it was scarcely a very dignified attitude for a government professing to be a strong government, to sit vacantly at the top of the political pole, like another feminine object of popular sport, and allow itself to be pelted contemptuously by rebels and murderers—to put itself upon a par with the Papal and Hellenic weakness which has made those countries a byword for executive incapacity throughout Europe. Sydney Smith, as we know, used to say that we should never be safe from railway accidents until a bishop was sacrificed in one; and it was curious to observe the wonderful energy displayed by the authorities, two or three years ago, when a Home

Secretary was threatened. Until some such stimulus to action is offered once more—until the present Chief Secretary, for instance, has the feeling of insecurity brought forcibly home to him in some such way—we are to continue, apparently, to behold that sorry spectacle of a government with its executive power absolutely paralyzed, and possessing about as much guiding power over the country, as the figurehead of a ship may pretend to. Mr. Gladstone, speaking of the land question, says, "we must not disguise from ourselves that the difficulty of this question has been aggravated by delay;" and yet he persistently disguises from himself the daily aggravation of lawlessness and outrage in Ireland, owing to the same unpardonable delay in putting the law in force. The leading journal tells us that we must trust to time, and the gradual operation of remedial measures; closing our ears, meanwhile, to the cries which go up from murdered homes, and taking no account of the miserable daily apprehension amid which men's lives are now passed in Ireland. But it declares at the same time, and has declared for months, with a dismal reiteration, that it *may* be necessary to show that a policy of justice is not inconsistent with a vigorous administration of the law. *Quousque tandem*, indeed—when will the time have come for the exhibition of this energetic vindication of the law, which has hitherto been in abeyance? How many victims more are required to satisfy the Minister's voracious humanity? Unfortunately this species of humanity, which shrinks from pressing too hard upon poor rebels and murderers, is not appreciated by the loyal and peaceable section of the community at whose expense it is indulged. A learned judge then implores proprietors and jurymen to stay in the country, and do their duty, that the Government will protect them. A most reassuring prospect, indeed, to judge from recent experience. Another learned judge tells a barrister to take no notice of threatening letters; to do his duty, and be shot if need be. Then a Cabinet Minister comes forward with a piteous expression of imbecility, and asks, "What are we to do? Pity our weakness, good people; and take upon yourselves the responsibility which you are paying us ostensibly to relieve you from." Even supposing it to be granted—which most unquestionably it is not—that there was a well-organized detective force in the country, and that it was impossible to obtain evidence to lead to a conviction of murderers—is it impossible to reach rebels, who are openly parading the streets with ostentatious sedition, and who at the very first sign of energy on the part of the executive shrink into silence at once ? Is it impossible to reach a murderous and seditious press, which is circulated unrestrained through the country, and which Englishmen, if they only had the slightest notion of its contents, never could allow the Government to encourage ? Is it impossible to limit the general sense of impunity which the permission of such elements of disorder serves to spread ? We are told that the Government is now going to the root of the whole question ; but has their experience tended to show them that the riotous element in Ireland, if dissatisfied—which they professedly are with the present Land Bill—will be one bit less active in future, or that we shall have any cessation from murder and riot as long as the Irishman has not got exactly what he wants, and what no Government will ever give him ? His love of justice is a mere myth—his love of prejudice and himself is his ruling passion, and as long as that is not satisfied he will agitate, and rebel, and murder to the end of the chapter, if he is not kept in order by the only power which has any influence with him—firmness. It is not to be wondered at that the desire for repeal should now be spreading through the country. If the English Government cannot protect them, people say, at least let them try to protect themselves. If the last Irish Parliament *was* a failure, it could hardly have been a more miserable failure than English rule at present is. One used to look upon the cry for repeal as emanating from a kind of fanatical patriotism, not worth wasting a thought upon : but now, when one sees the Imperial Government playing into the hands of repealers by a display of weakness and hesitation and incapacity which is alienating all the class whose lives are daily endangered in consequence ; and when one sees that Hungary, by reason of her importunity, has gained a similar point with Austria, and that the New Zealand colonists are being left to manage *their* barbarians by themselves, one cannot help thinking that the Irish colonists, too, will one day be allowed to take in hand for themselves the remnant of savagery which civilization has not yet crushed into extinction, and that we *shall* some day have security for life, and some sort of law and order in Ireland.

THE END.

London : Printed by SMITH, ELDER and Co., Old Bailey, E.C.

www.ingramcontent.com/pod-product-compliance
Lightning Source LLC
Chambersburg PA
CBHW032102230426
43672CB00009B/1608